Foreword

"Death and life are in the power of the tongue; those who love it will eat its fruit." This powerful scripture resonates deeply with me and encapsulates the essence of Dr. Digna Wheatley Pearson's book, Crown of Life Confessions. A steadfast believer in the transformative power of our words, Dr. Wheatley Pearson encourages us to declare victorious confessions over our lives, families, communities, and the world.

Though we attended the same high school, our true connection blossomed later in life through prayer and friendship. Digna is an active member of Spirit of Faith Christian Center, now Faith City Central, a word-of-faith ministry that underscores the significance of confessions. Over the years, I have witnessed her faith and spoken declarations become a reality.

Life often throws unexpected challenges our way, leading us to moments of despair and disappointment. In the wake of her husband's and parents' transitions, Digna began crafting her own confessions to reinforce God's word in her life. This practice not only fortified her faith but also helped her navigate through dark times when surrendering to despair would have been easier. Are you yearning for change? Have your prayers felt unanswered, leaving you longing for a breakthrough?

Victory resides in your words. This manual is designed to empower you to reclaim authority over your life through confessions.

As an author, speaker, wellness coach, and, most importantly, a child of the Most High God, I encourage you to transform your speech to align with your desired walk. I trust that the Lord and Savior, Jesus Christ, will honor your faith-filled confessions as you delight in Him. Your first confession can be a simple acknowledgment of Jesus' birth, death, burial, and resurrection, inviting Him to be your Savior and Lord. If you're not quite there yet, rest assured that you're in my prayers for a fuller experience of life as you engage with these confessions. May you find comfort, encouragement, and strength within these pages.

This book is not merely an ornament for your bookshelf or coffee table; it is a transformative tool. When you purchase Crown of Life Confessions, commit to reading it, believing it, declaring it, and witnessing its activation in your life. The universe was spoken into existence by our Father God—what are you creating in your own world? Having had the privilege of reviewing this book prior to its publication, I can attest that Crown of Life Confessions is a formidable weapon for achieving victory. I was inspired to continue confessing the Word!

It is with great honor that I endorse this book and invite you to make it a vital part of your journey.

Tisha Lynton Rose

Dedication

This book is dedicated to Spirit of Faith Christian Center, now Faith City Central, which taught me about the Spirit of Faith. Through this ministry, I have exercised my faith and witnessed the miraculous in numerous circumstances. These faith principles changed the trajectory of my life. I am who I am because of the instructions I chose to follow, and I imitate those who, through faith and patience, inherited the promises. And since we have the same spirit of faith, according to what is written, "I believed and therefore I spoke," we also believe and therefore speak (2 Corinthians 4:13).

Table of Contents

Introduction 19

Worship the Lord 29

    Adoration 29

    Exaltation 30

    Praise The Lord 31

    Desiring Closeness with God 32

    Meditating In Your Word 33

    Confidence In God's Word 33

    Confidence In God 34

    The Power of The Spoken Word 34

    Adoration How Excellent Is Your Name 35

    Extravagant Love 36

    The Cost of the Oil In My Alabaster Box 37

Covering the Man/Woman of God 39

    The Good Shepherd 39

    Honoring the Man and Woman of God 40

    Helping Hands for the Pastors 41

    Equipping the Church 41

    The Power of God's Word 42

    Stir Up The Gift/Ignite the Anointing 43

    The Lord's Favor 43

Responding to the Call 45

    Fulfilling My Purpose 45

    Responding to the Calling 46

    This is the Way; Walk In It 48

    Here I Am, Send Me 48

    Your Words Are Spirit and Life 50

    Honor - The Divine Order of God 50

    Displaying The Fruit Of The Spirit 51

    A Fragrant Life 52

    Living Holy And Righteous 53

    A Good Name 54

Who AM I 55

    My Tongue is the Pen of a Ready Writer 55

    Kingdom Jurisdiction 57

    Arise And Shine 57

    Clothed With Strength 58

    Beautiful And Beloved 59

    I AM A Fearless Lioness 59

    I AM A King, A Prophet, A Priest 60

    I AM A Mighty Warrior 61

    I AM A Mighty Man of God 62

    I AM A Fighter 63

Wholeness of Body, Soul, and Mind 65
    Health and Healing 65
    Send Your Word 65
    Spiritual Vitality 66
    Long Life 66
    Long Healthy Life 67
    Old Age 68
    Healthy Lifestyle 68

Confidence Fully Rooted In God 71
    Divinely Designed Woman 71
    Divinely Designed Man 71
    Overcoming Insecurity 72
    Confidence In My Physical Appearance 73

Children Are A Gift From God 75
    When Desiring a Baby 75
    Overcoming Barrenness 76
    Desire For Children 76
    Fruitfulness 77
    Raising Godly Children 77
    Praying For Prodigal Children 78
    Prayer and Declarations For An Ill Child 79

Family Confessions **81**

    Family Treaty 81

    God-Fearing Family 81

    Unity in the Family 82

    Children 83

    Young King Confession 84

    Beloved Daughter Confession 85

Love Never Fails **87**

    Love 87

    A Woman Desiring A Marriage 87

    True Love 88

    A Woman Desiring A Mate 89

    Desiring Marriage/Sexual Purity 89

    A Man Desiring Marriage 90

God's Design For Marriage **93**

    The Pillars of Marriage 93

    Covenant Love 95

    Walking in Love 95

    Forgiveness 96

Overcoming Sickness And Disease **99**

    Arthritis 99

    Alzheimer's And Dementia 100

    Brain Fog……………………………………………………………… 101

    Fighting Cancer……………………………………………………… 102

    Healing From Diseases…………………………………………… 103

    Distress………………………………………………………………… 108

    Complete Recovery From All Types of Cancer……………… 108

    Quicken My Mortal Body………………………………………… 109

    Physical, Mental, and Spiritual Disciplines………………… 109

    Headaches and Migraines……………………………………… 111

    Recovering From A Stroke……………………………………… 112

    Victory Over Stress-Related Fatigue………………………… 114

Miracle Manifestations………………………………………………….. 117

    Miracle Manifestations…………………………………………… 117

    Pick Up Your Mat And Walk…………………………………… 118

Security and Protection…………………………………………………. 119

    The Full Armor of God…………………………………………… 119

    An Ever-Present Help……………………………………………… 120

        Accidents……………………………………………………… 120

    Help Me Lord………………………………………………………… 121

    Enemies………………………………………………………………… 121

    The Angel of the Lord…………………………………………… 122

    Touch Not My Anointed………………………………………… 122

    Protection From My Enemies………………………………… 123

Anoint My Head In My Enemies' Presence 124

Divine Protection While Traveling 125

God's Divine Protection 126

The Lord is My Shepherd 127

The Choice Weapon of My Warfare 127

Restoration And Renewal 129

Refreshing Others 129

Transformation 130

Suddenly 130

Broken Chains 131

Remove The Veil Sealed To The Day Of Redemption 131

The Fountain of Living Waters 133

New Heaven And New Earth 134

Victory Through Christ 135

Triumph Over Mental Challenges 137

Stress and Anxiety 137

When Feeling Overwhelmed 137

Exhaustion and Stress 138

Worry and Anxiety 138

Pride 139

Overcoming Intimidation and Fear 140

Anxiety 141

    Overcoming Stinking Thinking.. 142

    Emotional Instability/ Unstable Mind................................. 144

    Overcoming Childhood Trauma and Bullying...................... 145

    Overcoming Trauma.. 146

    Breaking The Curse... 146

Conquering Anger, Bitterness, Resentment, Guilt and Shame.. 149

    Guarding My Heart... 149

    Overcoming The Root of Bitterness and Resentment......... 150

    Seeking Forgiveness... 150

    Dealing with Oppression.. 151

    Overcoming Rejection..152

    Addressing Shame and Guilt.. 153

    No More Condemnation... 154

Triumph Over Grief, Loss, and Mourning..........................157

    Overcoming Grief and Loss..157

    Overcoming Grief and Mourning..158

    Overcoming Painful Thoughts of Despair and Discouragement 159

    Dominion Over Depression...160

Overwhelming Peace...163

    Peace.. 163

    Peace is A Firm Foundation.. 164

Victory Over the Storm 165

Watch Your Mouth 167

Anger 167

Set A Guard Over My Mouth 168

Unwholesome Talk 169

Financial Victory 171

Financial Increase 171

A Wise Steward 171

Provision 172

Sowing 173

Possessing My Promised Land 173

Prosperity 174

Tithing 175

Stewardship 176

Millionaire Confession 177

Guaranteed Financial Security 178

The Power to Get Wealth 179

The Blessing of Hard Work 179

Generosity 180

Financial Legacy 181

The Blessing of the Lord 181

Supernatural Breakthrough 182

    Harvest 183

    Financial Provision 184

    Exceeding Abundant Blessing 184

Deciding On The Right Course of Action 185

    Decision Making 185

    Wavering Faith 186

    Hearing From God 186

    Guidance From The Holy Spirit 187

    Not Leaning to My Own Understanding 188

    Waiting On God 189

    The Will of God For My Life 190

    Character Development 191

    Career Choices 192

    Purchasing Land/Building A Home 193

    Timing Is Everything 194

    Trusting God While Waiting 195

    Move Forward 196

Discerning Truth From Error/Right From Wrong 199

    The Gift of Discernment 199

    The Spirit of Discernment 200

    Spiritual Wisdom 201

    Speak To My Heart Lord 201

Revelation.. 202

Avoiding Naïve Decision-making.. 203

The Benefits of Wisdom.. 204

Choosing The Right Alliances... 205

Healthy Friendships... 206

Order My Footsteps.. 207

Obedience... 207

Cultivating A Spirit of Humility...208

Persistent Confident Prayer...209

Filled With All Knowledge, Spiritual Wisdom, And Understanding... 210

Delay In Answered Prayer.. 210

Discerning The Will of God.. 211

Blessings Upon Blessings... 213

World Changer Leadership.. 213

Anointing.. 214

Bearing Fruit/Equipped For Success................................. 215

Business Success.. 216

Marketplace Ministry Anointing....................................... 217

Starting A Successful Business.. 219

Managing Business Growth.. 221

Surrounded By Favor... 222

Blessings For The Righteous/Favor................................... 223

- Chosen Instrument Pursuing Purpose 224
- Chosen And Handpicked By God 224
- Promotion 225
- Victorious Life 225
- Acceleration 226
- Perpetual Victory 227

Addressing Fear **229**
- Meditation 229
- My Encompassing Shield 230
- 911 (Psalms 91) 230
- I AM Victorious 231
- The Faith Fight 232
- Seeking God's Protection 233
- When I'm Afraid/Fearful And Need Protection 233
- A Kingdom That Can't Be Shaken/Unshakeable Kingdom 234
- Casting My Care 235
- Facing Trials 236
- Victory Over The Storm 237
- Speak to the Storm 238
- Peace in the Storm 239
- Overcoming Fear 240
- Shake it Off 241

Overcoming The Fear of Death.. 242

A Resilient Spirit.. **245**

Joy Is My Weapon 245

The Strong Spirit Of A Man.. 246

Strength.. 247

Pillar of Strength.. 248

The Joy of the Lord Is My Strength.. 248

The Crown of Life/The Victor's Crown..................................... 249

Firmly Rooted... 249

Remaining Strong In Crisis.. 250

Finishing Strong: A Caregiver's Confession........................... 251

Sweet Sleep.. **255**

Sweet Sleep.. 255

Rest For The Weary.. 255

Waiting On God.. 256

Victory In Court Cases... **259**

The Nation.. **261**

Healing The Nations... 261

Praying For Our Educational Institutions And
Schools... 265

The Incarcerated And Imprisoned.. 266

A Fire Fighter's Confession... 268

A Police Officer's Confession.. 269

A Military Soldier's Confession.. 271

A Healthcare Worker's Confession.. 273

The Political System Confession.. 275

A Fight To The Finish... 276

Bonus Confession... 279

Receive Jesus As Your Savior.. 283

Receive Holy Spirit... 285

Biblical Sources.. 287

References... 288

Books By The Author... 289

About The Author.. 290

Contact Information.. 291

Introduction

Proverbs 18:21, Amplified Version, says, "Death and life are in the power of the tongue, And those who love it and indulge in it will eat its fruit and bear the consequences of their words." Did this scripture evoke a strong emotional response when you read it? It did for me and helped me to realize how much power and authority I have over my life when I speak.

Your speech has the capacity or ability to direct or influence the behavior or course of events in your life. If you speak negatively, you will receive a negative harvest. If you speak positively, you will reap a positive and favorable harvest. Scripture warns us to "avoid all perverse talk; stay away from corrupt speech." (NLT. Prov. 4:24) Wow! Let me say that backward, wow! When we speak words that are not life-giving or uplifting, it is perverse. Merriam-Webster defines "perverse" as something improper, incorrect, opposing what is right, reasonable, accepted, or wrongheaded, arising from stubbornness or obstinacy and turning away from what is right or good. Do you need more convincing about the power of your words?

Job exemplifies someone who had a consistently negative confession about his children. Regularly, Job said, "It may be that my sons have sinned and cursed God in their hearts." (NKJV, Job 1:5). Unfortunately, all of Job's children died, and he experienced greater loss, including all of his possessions, wealth, and experienced an attack on his health. Yet, Job said, "Teach me, and I will hold my tongue; cause me to understand wherein I have erred. How forceful are right words!" (NKJV, Job 6:24-25).

In Numbers 13, we find another example of a negative confession. The Israelites refused to enter the promised land, saying, "We are not able to go up against the people, for they are stronger than we." And they gave the children of Israel a bad report of the land they had spied out, saying, "The land through which we have gone as spies is a land that devours its inhabitants, and all the people whom we saw in it are men of great stature. There we saw the giants (the descendants of Anak came from the giants), and we were like grasshoppers in our own sight, and so we were in their sight." (NKJV, Num. 13:31-33). This negative confession resulted in the Israelites dying in the wilderness because they did not believe God and His promises to them. God said, "They certainly shall not see the land of which I swore to their fathers, nor shall any of those who rejected Me see it." (NKJV, Num. 14:23) The Israelites failed to set a guard over their mouths and keep watch over the door of their lips.

Not speaking faith-filled words resulted in devastating outcomes for the Israelites. The words that come out of your mouth have the power to completely change your circumstances and alter the course of your life. In other words, you have set a trap for yourself by your spoken words. The bible describes it as "ensnared" by the words of your mouth. Your speech will position you in a situation that is difficult or impossible to escape. Place a guard over your tongue and speak the right words. There's a promise, power, and anointing upon God's word to uproot everything you have ever spoken over your life for years. You can, of course, course-correct and change the trajectory of your life.

In Genesis, we find the creation story: "In the beginning, God created the heavens and the earth. The earth was without form and void, and darkness was on the face of the deep. And God began to speak. Every time God spoke, something manifested:

- **Then God said,** "Let there be light," and there was light. (v. 5)
- **Then God said,** "Let there be a firmament in the midst of the waters and let it divide the waters from the waters. (v. 6)
- **Then God said,** "Let the waters under the heavens be gathered together into one place, and let the dry land appear," and it was so. (v. 9)
- **Then God said,** "Let the earth bring forth grass, the herb that yields seed, and the fruit

tree that yields fruit according to its kind, whose seed is in itself, on the earth," and it was so. (v. 11)

- **Then God said,** "Let there be lights in the firmament of the heavens to divide the day from the night; and let them be for signs and seasons, and for days and years, and let them be for lights in the firmament of the heavens to give light on the earth"; and it was so. (v. 14-15).
- **Then God said,** "Let the waters abound with an abundance of living creatures and let birds fly above the earth across the face of the firmament of the heavens." (v. 20).
- **Then God said,** "Let the earth bring forth the living creature according to its kind: cattle and creeping thing and beast of the earth, each according to its kind," and it was so. (v. 24)
- **Then God said,** "Let Us make man in Our image, according to Our likeness; let them have dominion over the fish of the sea, over the birds of the air, and over the cattle, over all the earth and over every creeping thing that creeps on the earth. (v. 26)
- **And God said,** "See, I have given You every herb that yields seed which is on the face of all the earth, and every tree whose fruit yields seed; to You, it shall be for food. (v. 29).

- "Then God **saw everything that He had made**, and indeed ***it was very good.***" (v. 31)

God, the ultimate Master Artist, used His words and imagination to create this universe and humanity. Similarly, you can be the master artist of your own life by speaking your vision into existence. You are a speaking spirit! When you decree a thing, it will manifest. The spoken word is a powerful instrument. Use it wisely. God says, "Today, I have given you the choice between life and death, between blessings and curses. Now, I call on heaven and earth to witness the choice you make. Oh, that you would choose life so that you and your descendants might live!" (NLT, Deut. 30:19) God encourages us to put Him in remembrance of His promises (NKJV, IS. 43:26). Remembering God's promises renews, reinforces, and strengthens our faith, especially when we are facing battles. One of my favorite promises of God is found in Joshua 23:14, "And you know in all your hearts and in all your souls that not one thing has failed of all the good things which the Lord Your God spoke concerning you. All have come to pass for you; not one word of them has failed (NKJV)." What a wonderful reminder about God's goodness toward us.

As believers, we must come into agreement with God's words. Dictionary.com defines agreement as the absence of incompatibility between two things. This means there's no conflict between the two individuals.

According to Hebrews 13:7, there's a consistency that runs through us all. Therefore, we always conduct ourselves as Christ would, and when we do, we consistently achieve the same level of success in everything we do. Jesus only does what the Father tells him to do and only speaks what His Father tells him to speak. "Most assuredly, I say to you, the Son can do nothing of Himself, but what He sees the Father do; for whatever He does, the Son also does in like manner." (John 5:19). Furthermore, For I have never spoken on My own initiative *or* authority, but the Father Himself who sent Me has given Me a commandment regarding what to say and what to speak." (John 12:49 AMP)

Apostle Fredrick K.C. Price said, "You will never live above your confession. Confession brings possession." You can have the mind and mouth of Christ by confessing the word of God, and it will allow the favor of God to expand exponentially in your life. God watches over His word to perform it (Jer. 1:12). When you decree a thing, it is established in the earth (Job 23:28). This is similar to Kings and Queens who issue royal decrees that their subjects must follow. We are part of the royal priesthood, a chosen people. In Mark 11:23, Jesus said, "Whoever says to this mountain, be removed and be cast into the sea and does not doubt in his heart, but believes that those things he says will be done, he will have whatever he says."

Confession will shift the atmosphere and bring the spirit of peace into all your relationships, whether at work, at home, at school, or wherever you may be. Confession allows you to apply pressure with God's word and experience God's supernatural move in your life. Lastly, words create a confident expectation. We call those things that be not as though they were. You have to see it before you possess it. Always practice speaking the Word of God. Your tongue is the pen of a ready writer, and the gates of hell shall not prevail against you.

The Benefits of Confessing the Word of God

- Ignites your faith (Rom. 10:8)
- Inspires your vision (Acts 2:17)
- Informs your conversations (1 Peter 1: 15-16)
- Improves your confidence in God's word (1 John 5:14)
- Increases your level of hope and expectation (Jer. 29:11)
- Inspires feelings of self-confidence, self-worth, and self-esteem (Gen. 1:26)
- Impacts your physical, emotional, and spiritual health immeasurably (Ps. 107:20)

The Regimen for Success

- Start slowly. The fastest runner doesn't always win the race. Gradually build up to at least 30 minutes of daily confession.
- Make it a daily routine. Making confessions should be a lifestyle.
- Find a convenient time and place to say your confessions where there are no distractions.
- Make it a daily habit, but remain flexible if you miss a day of doing your confessions. The goal is to make confessions a gradual, consistent daily practice.
- Don't get discouraged
- Encourage others to join you. Make it fun.
- Keep a journal to document your progress and victories as they start to manifest.
- Remember, you can change your life by speaking God's word daily.

Walk with Christ Daily

Develop a dependence on Christ so you can experience total breakthroughs in your life. Jesus desires to commune with you daily. As a result, He will direct and guide you in all that you do. According to Jeremiah 17:7, "Blessed [with spiritual security] is the man who believes and trusts in and relies on the Lord And whose hope and confident expectation is the Lord." What a beautiful promise for the believer. God has loved you and drawn you with an everlasting love, and with loving kindness. We cultivate our relationship with Christ through:

- Daily pray
- Meditating on God's word
- Engaging in praise and worship
- Praying in your heavenly language (Praying in tongues)
- Walking in faith and love towards others by avoiding strife in your life.

Jesus loves you and cares for you. So, let's get started!

Worship the Lord

Adoration

Hosana, Hosana! I exalt thee, O Lord! Yahweh, Yahweh, I will bless the Lord, oh my soul, with all that is within me. I bless Your Holy name! You are worthy of praise, for You are the living God and the God who performs signs, wonders, and miracles. You are King of Kings and Lord of Lords. You are Holy. Your name is beautiful. No one compares to You. I praise Your great and awesome name. I worship and bow down before You. I kneel before my Lord and Maker.

You reign above all the earth, and I make a joyful noise to You, oh Lord, over all the earth. I serve You with gladness, and I come into Your presence with singing. I enter Your gates with thanksgiving and Your courts with praise. I bless Your name for You, Lord, are good, and Your steadfast love endures forever and ever, and Your faithfulness to all generations. I exalt the Lord my God and worship at Your footstool! Holy are You!

I sing to You. I sing praises to You; I tell of all Your wondrous works! I glory in Your holy name; My heart seeks You, Lord, and I rejoice! I lift You High, Yahweh. I give thanks to You, oh Lord; I call upon Your name and make known Your deeds among all the people! I sing to You. I sing praises to You and tell of all Your wondrous works! I glory in Your holy name. My heart rejoices as I seek the Lord. I rejoice! I proclaim the excellencies of Your name because You called me out of darkness into Your marvelous light. I continually offer a sacrifice of praise to You with the fruit of my lips, acknowledging Your name.

Scriptures: Ps. 103:1; Ps. 99:1-5; Ps. 100:1-5; Ps. 95:6; 1 Pet. 2:9; Heb. 13:15

Exaltation

I will extol You, my God and my King, and I will bless Your name forever and ever. Every day, I will bless You and praise Your name continually. Great are You, Lord, and greatly to be praised, and Your greatness is unsearchable. I live to praise You, God. You are Yahweh. You are Elohim. You are Adonai.

Lord, anoint me with the oil of gladness until it overflows. Your joy is my strength, Lord. I rejoice in the shadow of Your wings. I rejoice exceedingly in Your presence. I am happy because You are my God.

I live to praise and exalt You. I lift Your Name, High, Yahweh - the I AM WHO I AM. The name above all names. You are Lord, Master, and Ruler, my Adonai. All the Glory and Honor belong to You. It's rightfully Yours. I worship and adore You. You are the most sovereign

God. There's nobody like You, and Your faithfulness endures forever.

Scriptures: Ps.145; Ps. 45:7; Ps. 21:1; Ps. 63:7; Ps. 144:15

Praise The Lord

Spirit of the Living God, I invite You into all the affairs of my life. You are the King of Glory, my wonderful, majestic God. I bow and worship You, Lord. I praise You, Lord, for Your goodness and mercy and all Your wonderful works to the children of men! You are my Commander in Chief, the Mighty Warrior who saves me from all my sorrows, worries, and troubles. You are my Strong Tower in danger, the one I run to when I need shelter from the storm. You are my hiding place and my shield. My Redeemer, who paid a precious, unimaginable price to buy my soul and spirit back from darkness.

Thank you for Your Beloved Son, who made the ultimate sacrifice on my behalf as the mediator of sin, the perfect Lamb of God. You are Alpha and Omega, the beginning and the end. The author and finisher of my faith, and I worship You, Lord, and I bow before You. You are the Bread of Life, the fountain of living waters, and the true vine that sustains my life. God with us, Immanuel, who promises never to leave me or forsake me. You even left the ninety-nine to come after and pursue me.

You are the Good Shepherd. I am grateful for Your persistence and passionate pursuit of me. You are the best Bridegroom who demonstrates unending, unfailing love. You are my rock and salvation, and I will not be moved from You because Your love for me never fails; You are the Way, the Truth, and the Life. As the Fountain of Living Water, You satisfy my soul, and I will never have to thirst again. Since You are the Prince of Peace, shalom resonates in every area of my life. I love You, Lord, and I promise to worship You forever!

Scriptures: Prov: 12:6; Matt. 15:29-31; Ps. 12:4

Desiring Closeness With God

You inhabit the praises of Your people. Fill me with Your Spirit, Lord. I hunger and thirst for righteousness. I am hungry for more of You. Father, allow me to experience Your glory. Do not hide Your face from me. I'm desperate for more of You. You said, If I seek You, I will find You when I search for You with all my heart. And when I am found by You, You will bring me back from my captivity and my bondage. Set me free, Lord. If You set me free, I will be free indeed. Forgive me, Lord, and be the Savior of my soul. Thank you for loving me, for forgiving me, and for saving me.

Scriptures: Ps. 23:3; Eph. 5:18; Matt. 5:6; Ps. 63; Jer. 29:13; Jn. 8:36

Meditating In Your Word

Father, I meditate on Your word because it is the prescription for a long, good, healthy, wealthy life. I keep Your words before my eyes daily. I do not let them depart from me. I meditate upon the scripture so that it takes root in my heart, bears fruit in my life, and overflows with health. This Book of the Law shall not depart from my mouth. I will meditate on it day and night. I will observe and do all that is written in it. Therefore, my way will be prosperous, and I will have good success.

Scriptures: Josh. 1:8; Ps. 1

Confidence in God's words

I stagger not at the promise of God through unbelief. I am strong in faith and give You glory. I am fully persuaded that what You promised, You will perform. You promise that whatever I desire when I pray, if I believe that I receive them, I shall have them. I believe that all Your promises are yes and amen. I refuse to look at the things that are seen but rather focus on the things that are not seen, for the things that are seen are temporal, but the things that are not seen are eternal. You have not given me a spirit of fear but of power, love, and a sound mind. I will hold fast to the profession of my faith without wavering because You are faithful who promised, and Your word will never return void unto You, but it will accomplish what You said it would do. Your track record is impeccable with me, and I trust You.

Scriptures: Rom. 4:20-23; Mark 11:24; 2 Cor. 1:20; 2 Cor. 4:18; 2 Tim. 1:7; Heb. 10:23; Is. 55:11

Confidence In God

I am blessed because I am a woman/man who trusts in the Lord. I have made the Lord my hope and confidence. I won't be impatient. I will wait for the Lord, and He will come and save me! I will be brave, stouthearted, and courageous. Yes, I will wait, and God will help me. I will not be a victim. I am a victor. For all creation eagerly awaits that future day when God will reveal who his children really are. As an adopted son and daughter of God, this is my birthright to be glorified with God.

Scriptures: Ps. 27:14; Rom. 8:19

The Power of The Spoken Word

Father, there's a promise, power, and anointing upon Your word. Lord, I know that You are greater than all gods. I have seen Your works in my life and in the lives of others. Because I have believed, please fulfill Your promises to me. Hasten Your word to perform it. So that things will happen so fast my head will swim.

Scriptures: Luke 1:45; Jer. 1:12; Amos 9:13-15; Rev. 2

Adoration, How Excellent Is Your Name

O Lord, my Lord, how excellent and majestic *is* Your name throughout all the earth. You deserve all the honor and the praise. Father, there is no comparison to Your greatness. Thank You for being my Lord and Savior. You are my unwavering strength, my shield, the horn of my salvation, my stronghold, and my defense. You are the mighty, mighty God. The creator of all the heavens and the earth. You reign as King over all the earth.

You are my shield, my source of help, and my joy. You are my solid rock. You have been so good to me, and I am overwhelmed. I thank You for all Your wonderful acts. At night, You counsel me and instruct my heart. My heart trusts in You completely, and You help me. My heart leaps and overflows with joy, knowing that You bear my burdens daily.

I rely heavily on You because You brought me from my mother's womb, and I proudly bear Your name. I will continually praise You. I will sing of Your love and justice; to You, LORD, I will sing of Your praises. You rescue me from the hands of the wicked. You are a shield to all who place their trust in You. When I cry, You respond and redeem me.

Who am I that You are mindful of me? You are the Father of Compassion and the God of all comfort. You have enriched my life with every spiritual blessing in Christ and in the heavenly realms. I live with great expectation and hope of eternal life because Christ rose again from the dead. You are my living hope. O Lord, my Lord, how majestic is Your name in all the earth!

Scriptures: Dan. 2:20; Exo. 15:2; Deut. 32:3; 2 Sam. 22:47; 1 Chron. 16:9; Ps.13:6; Ps.16:7; Ps. 21:13; Ps. 28:7; Ps. 47:7; Ps.71:6; Ps. 101:1; Luke 1:68; Ps. 68:19; 2 Cor. 1:3; Jer. 20:13; Eph. 1:3; Ps. 8; Ps. 18; Ps. 101:1

Extravagant Love

Your extravagant love kept You on the cross for me. Thank you for placing Your son and Your passion on the line when I was weak and rebellious. That's the ultimate sacrifice. You found me worthy of dying for. I am deeply grateful for Your selfless love and sacrifice and for choosing to adopt me into Your own family, for it brings You immense joy and pleasure. You chose me before the foundation of the world so that I would be holy, consecrated, set apart for You, purpose-driven, and blameless in Your sight. As a child of God, I am securely transformed by Your incredible works of love. Thank you for Your endless love, mercy, grace, goodness, and forgiveness.

All the glory belongs to You. So, I praise You, God, for the glorious, magnificent grace You poured out on me. I commit to doing the will of the Father as a chosen vessel from the foundation of the world, from my mother's womb, to serve in Your Kingdom and fulfill Your divine purpose on earth. I am made alive by Your Spirit. You are the author and finisher of my faith.

Blessed and worthy of praise be the God and Father of my Lord Jesus Christ, who has blessed me with every spiritual blessing in the heavenly realms in Christ.

Scriptures: Rom. 5:8; Eph. 1:3-6; 1 Pet. 3:18; Heb. 12:2

The Cost of the Oil in My Alabaster Box

Father, You reign in my heart forever. You are holy and unchanging for all eternity. I worship You in spirit and truth. My love for You is extravagant and knows no bounds. I earnestly desire to please You and honor You with my life. Throughout my childhood, I've been judged and misunderstood. These experiences led to much pain, hurt, embarrassment, humiliation, rejection, sadness, depression, and brokenness. Yet, I choose to exchange my past pain for Your perfect peace, Your shalom. I refuse to settle for anything less than complete wholeness, health, and prosperity in every area of my life, knowing that You desire the best for me. Thank you for the immense price You paid for me. I am deeply grateful. The cost of Your oil pales in comparison to my sacrifice. As a precious, extravagant gift, I lay my hopes and dreams at Your feet. I worship at Your feet, Jesus, so the oil in my alabaster box can flow freely. I surrender all that I am to You.

Scripture: Matt. 26:6-13

Covering the Man and Woman of God

The Good Shepherd

God, thank You for my pastor, who is a shepherd after Your own heart. My pastor teaches the Word with simplicity, wisdom, and understanding. Pastor ____ serves faithfully, is wise, and leads well. Pastor_____ is prepared in season and out of season. Pastor _____ appropriately corrects, rebukes, and encourages us with great patience and careful instruction. My pastor awakens my spirit and soul when he/she teaches with simplicity. My pastor watches over my soul and all the flock given to him by the Holy Spirit.

Help my pastor to remain above reproach, sober-minded, self-controlled, respectable, hospitable, and the husband/wife of one person. My pastor is not a drunkard, given to violence, or quarrelsome. Gentleness permeates their spirit. My pastor is not a lover of money but a good steward of everything God provides.

Watch over my pastor's family. Help Pastor _____ to manage his/her household well. Place a hedge of protection around them that prevents the devil from entering their lives and wreaking havoc. Defend my pastor and his family. Encourage my pastor's children to be well-behaved and not run away from the calling upon their lives. May my pastor's family help him by serving in ministry as well. Protect Pastor_____from evil. Help my pastor with their eye and ear gate.

Please help me to honor my pastor in thought, word, and deed. Moreover, please assist me in keeping my mouth from speaking evil or ill of my pastor and their family. My pastor can count on me because I am a faithful servant in the church who pushes the God-given vision.

Scriptures: Jer. 3:15; 2 Tim. 3:16-17; Heb. 13:17; 1 Tim. 3: 1-7

Honoring the Man and Woman of God

Pastor_____ preaches and teaches God's Word, and their life reflects the Word of God that they teach. When I examine their life closely, their faithfulness and truthfulness instruct me. I obey my spiritual leaders and recognize their authority. Pastor_____ keeps watch over my soul because they must give an account to God for me. I follow the example. I will not be a heavy burden to my pastor. I come alongside and lift up my pastor's arms so we can win, and the enemy does not prevail against us.

Signs, wonders, and miracles are proof of my pastor's apostleship. Pastor____ is with me through good and bad times, encouraging me to persevere, not quit and give up. I honor and respect the doors of opportunity they have opened for me and the increase it has brought to my life. I respect and honor my pastors, and because they model the message, they should be paid well and receive double honor for faithfully preaching and teaching the revelation of the Word of God.

Scriptures: Heb. 3:17; Exo. 17:12-14; Ps. 20:8; James 1:12; 1 Tim. 5:17

Helping Hands for the Pastors

When I feel overwhelmed, I look to the Lord. He is the source of my help. Sometimes, I feel overwhelmed, burnt out, and stressed out with all my responsibilities. The work can feel too heavy at times. Send good help so I don't have to handle it alone. Thank you for the Aarons and Hurs who will provide the rock for me to sit on, stand beside me, and hold up my arms, keeping them steady and guaranteeing our victory.

Scriptures: Ps. 121:1; Exo. 17:12-14

Equipping the Church

And God gave some to be apostles, some prophets, some evangelists, and some pastors and teachers, for the equipping of the saints for the work of the ministry, for the edifying of the body of Christ, till we all come to the unity of the faith and the knowledge of the Son of God, to a perfect man, to the measure of the stature of the fullness of Christ.

Father, thank you for these special messengers and representatives who speak a new message from God to the people, spreading the good news of salvation and shepherding, guiding, and instructing them to fully equip and perfect the saints for the works of service that build up the body of Christ. As a result, I will grow spiritually, becoming a mature believer who reaches the fullness of Christ by exercising my spiritual gifts.

Scriptures: Eph. 4:11-16; Mark 16:15

The Power Of God's Word

The unfolding of Your words gives light and understanding to the simple. The word of God is alive, active, powerful, energizing, and effective. It is sharper than the sharpest two-edged sword, cutting between the soul and spirit, between the joints and marrow. It exposes my innermost thoughts and desires. Your laws are perfect, reviving the soul. Your word is spirit, and it is life. Your testimony is sure, making the simple wise. I love You, Lord, and I will keep Your word, and as my Father, You will love me and come to me and make Your home with me.

Scriptures: Eph 4:11-13; Ps. 119:130; Ps. 19:7; John 14:23; John 6:63

Stir Up the Gift/Ignite the Anointing

Empower me to impart Your Word to Your people. Let Your healing anointing flow through my hands, bringing spiritual, mental, emotional, physical, and financial deliverance, transforming every aspect of their lives. Use me as Your appointed and anointed instrument, igniting the gifts, talents, calling, and abilities You've bestowed upon me for Your glory. Stir up the gift. Ignite the anointing.

Scriptures: 2 Tim 1:16

The Lord's Favor

The Spirit of the Sovereign Lord is on me because the Lord has anointed me to proclaim the good news to the poor. He has sent me to bind up the brokenhearted, to proclaim freedom for the captives, and release from darkness for the prisoners; to proclaim the year of the Lord's favor and day of vengeance of our God; to comfort all who mourn; and provide for those who grieve, to bestow on them a crown of beauty instead of ashes, the oil of joy instead of mourning, and a garment of praise instead of a spirit of despair. They will be called oaks of righteousness, a planting of the Lord for the display of His splendor.

Scripture: Is: 61:1-3

Responding to the Call

Fulfilling My Purpose

Father, for such a time as this have You, You have called me to the kingdom. I am willing to respond immediately to Your call, just like the disciples, regardless of my age. Use me as You have used Joseph, Moses, and Rahab despite their shortcomings. Help me trust You, even when I don't have all the details, including walking away from anything that may hinder my calling. When I feel inadequate, remind me that You will never leave me nor forsake me, but You will empower me to carry out Your plans. Encourage me like You did Moses and Gideon. Grant me the strength to endure challenges and opposition and empower my children to handle any bullying or teasing because of my decision to follow You.

Please, help me not to run away from the calling on my life, like Jonah did. I am a mighty woman/man of valor who will perform signs, wonders, and miracles, confirming that You are with me. I speak with authority and power when You put Your words in my mouth. Give me detailed instructions as You gave Noah, and help me so I can follow Your instructions to the smallest detail without any modification.

Father, although fulfilling this calling on my life may involve agony, suffering, distress, heartbreak, and pain, I am steadfast in my commitment to You. "Father, if it is Your will, You can take this cup away from me; nevertheless, not My will, but Yours, be done." I reaffirm my unwavering commitment to You. Please send angels to strengthen me. I need Your help to endure and remain resilient.

Grant me favor with everyone I encounter. Help me seek Your guidance, interpret dreams, and avoid moral failures. I will establish boundaries, pray, fast, and maintain accountability. Help me to be sensitive to Your voice, like Samuel, and to be a trustworthy, faithful servant after Your own heart. Give me wisdom and discernment to fulfill Your will in the earth. Here I am; send me.

Scriptures: 1 Sam. 3; 1 Kings 3:9; Is. 6:8; Esther 4:14; Deut. 31:8; Judg. 6:12; Jonah 1-4; 2 Cor. 12:12; Jer. 1:9; Gen. 6; Luke 22.

Responding to the Calling

Father, regardless of my age, I will respond immediately to Your call like the disciples. God, just like You used Joseph, an arrogant child, Moses, a murderer, and Rahab, a prostitute, use me too. Give me wisdom, discernment, and spiritual guidance to fulfill Your will on the earth.

Father, help me trust You even though I am not clear where You are calling me to. I need strength like Abraham, who walked away from his family. Point out anyone I want to bring with me who might hinder my progress, my goals, my destiny, and my destination. I should have made more progress and achieved more in life by now. I can't tolerate further impediments, obstacles, or obstructions to my journey and goals. When my self-confidence is low, and I feel inadequate to accomplish this call, encourage me as You did, Moses and Gideon.

Walk alongside me and never leave me or forsake me. I will not run away from the calling upon my life, as Jonah did. Since I decided to follow You, I need Your help to endure ridicule, mockery, and scorn. Help me empower my children to persevere against bullying and teasing. Let my children also embrace and support my calling.

Even when I make mistakes due to naivety, grant me favor with everyone I encounter. Father, give me dreams with the gift of interpretation that will result in promotion for me and my family, just like You did for Joseph and Daniel. Please help me to avoid moral failures that scatter the flock/the sheep. Help me establish guardrails that prevent me from failing. I will consistently pray and fast, maintain armor bearers at all times, engage in immediate repentance when I sin, ensure that I have accountability partners, and maintain spiritual covering.

Help me not to lose the supernatural strength You give me. Help me to always be sensitive to Your voice, just like Samuel. Speak, Lord, for Your servant hears. I am listening. I am a servant after Your own heart. I will worship, obey, and serve You wholeheartedly to fulfill Your purpose on earth. Here I am, send me.

Scriptures: 1 Kings 3:9; Gen. 12; Judges 6; Deut. 31:6-8; 1 Sam. 2; Acts 13:22; Is. 6:8; Gen. 41; Dan. 2

This Is The Way; Walk In It

When You stand at the door and knock, I hear Your voice, and I open the door and invite You in. I will hear and listen to what You speak and receive the assurances of peace You give me when You answer my prayer. And whether I turn to the right or the left, I will hear Your voice behind me, saying, "This is the way; walk in it." Change the trajectory of my life in a great, mighty, and powerful way with Your guidance and encouragement.

Scriptures: Rev. 3:20; Ps. 85; Heb. 4:12; Is. 30:21

Here I Am, Send Me

Father, I stand ready to respond immediately to Your call, regardless of my age, just like the disciples. Use me as You have used Joseph, Moses, and Rahab despite their flaws and limitations. Please help me to trust You and walk away from anything hindering my calling and purpose. When I feel inadequate and doubt my ability, remind me that You will never leave or forsake me; instead, empower me to carry out Your divine plans.

Your words, divine guidance, and purpose for me ignite a fire within me —a burning passion that cannot be extinguished. I am exhausted from trying to hold it in. I can no longer ignore the call. Like clay in the potter's hand, I submit to Your will, remaining pliable for Your highest use and purpose. I surrender to the calling to fulfill Your purpose on the earth so the light of the good news, the radiant glory of the Anointed One who is the very image of God, may shine brightly upon Your people. I will not concern myself with their faces for fear of approval, rejection, or disapproval.

Fill my heart and my mouth with Your words so I may uproot, tear down, destroy, and rebuild. Grant me the knowledge and wisdom needed to become a valuable vessel in this world, to carry out the unique plan You have for my life. I desire to please you. Here I am, Lord, send me! And I will faithfully execute Your divine plan on the earth.

Scriptures: Is. 6:8; Deut. 31:6-8; Ps. 85:8; I Sam. 3:8-9; 1 Kings 3:9; 1 Sam. 13:14; Phil 4:13; Is. 41:10; Prov. 22:6; Jer. 1:8-10; Jer. 18:2-6; Jer. 20:9

Your Words Are Spirit and Life

Lord, the words that You speak unto me are spirit, and they are life. You said, call to You, and You will answer me, and You will tell me great, mighty, and hidden things which I do not know and understand and cannot distinguish. Your word is a lamp to my feet and a light to my path. You said, "If I pay close attention to what I hear and listen carefully, greater understanding will You give me—and I will receive even more. I am Your sheep, and I hear Your voice. You know me, and I follow You. I thank You for the Helper, the Holy Spirit, who will teach me all things and bring to my remembrance all that You have said to me. I will be quick to hear, slow to speak, and slow to anger so I can experience victory and fulfill the plan and purpose You have for my life.

John 6:63; Jer. 33:3; Ps. 85:8; Ps. 119:105; Mark 4:24; John 10:27; John 14:26; Heb. 4:12; James 1:19

Honor - The Divine Order of God

It's God's desire that I honor everyone I encounter, regardless of my personal feelings, opinions, or whether I like or agree with them. I honor their position and authority because they are God's servants appointed by Him. I honor those in authority by praying for them diligently because the divine order aligns with His purpose for us. I examine my motives to ensure that I honor all people, as they have been created in God's image. As God's representative on earth, they deserve recognition, time, effort, attention, appreciation, respect, and interest.

I will outdo others in showing honor to those in authority, especially my parents, because God promises a long life. When I honor others, I honor God. My parents and those in authority may not have been perfect and may have even treated me poorly, but I choose to honor them anyway because God is duty-bound to protect and reward me. Honor transforms, heals, and restores my relationships. A culture of honor will reside in my home, workplace, and place of worship as it will shape my lifestyle and future. It leads to my personal growth and deepens my connections with others. Honor acts as a powerful catalyst, unlocking a flow of miraculous events, extraordinary signs, and awe-inspiring wonders.

Scriptures: 1 Pet. 2:17: Rom. 13:1-7; Rom. 12:10; Exo 20:12; Gen. 1:27; Eph. 6:2-3

Displaying the Fruit of the Spirit

God is the tree, and I am the branches. I am rooted in Christ; therefore, I will grow and bear good fruit in my life, such as love, joy, peace, patience, kindness, goodness, faithfulness, gentleness, and self-control. God is love, and the one who abides in love abides in God. Therefore, God abides continually in me.

I have embraced this love walk, heart, soul, and mind. I am reminded that love is patient and kind. It does not envy or boast; it is not proud. It does not dishonor others; it is not self-seeking. It is not easily angered, and it keeps no record of wrongs. Love does not delight in evil but rejoices with the truth. It always protects, trusts, hopes, and perseveres.

Scriptures: John 15; Gal. 5:22-23; 1 John 4; 1 Cor. 13.

A Fragrant Life

My consistent relationship with You fills me with unshakeable joy continually. Even when life's challenges and hardships arise, I find strength knowing that You are the God of hope who fills me with all joy and peace. As I trust in You, I can overflow with hope by the power of the Holy Spirit. When my mind remains firm, steadfast, solid, fixed, steady, and unwavering, constantly on You, You keep me in perfect peace.

I commit to being patient with everyone that I meet, never growing weary in doing good. I trust that if I remain steadfast, I will reap a harvest in due time. By making allowances for others' faults and mistakes, I demonstrate my love and foster a spirit of kindness and tenderheartedness. Surely goodness and mercy shall follow me all the days of my life, and I will dwell in the house of the Lord forever because faithful people abound in blessings.

My gentleness will shine through in all my interactions. I will be like Christ, offering a gentle touch, constant reassurance, and a caring hand. Gentleness will exude from my pores, drawing others to me because of the trust and respect I extend to them. I exercise self-control and discipline in every area of my life, which serves as a shield and a safeguard against the enemy. With all my heart, I joyfully celebrate others when I grow and exhibit the fruit of the Spirit.

Scriptures: Rom. 15:13; Is. 26:3; Gal. 6:9; Prov. 11:17; Eph. 4:32; Eph. 4:2; Ps. 23:6; Prov. 28:20; Phil. 4:5; Prov. 25:28

Living Holy and Righteous

I belong to God, and I am an integral part of God's divine plan. I have chosen to be no longer a slave to impurity and uncleanness or the ever-increasing wickedness and lawlessness around me. Instead, I have chosen to be a slave to righteousness, leading to holiness. God has a purpose for everyone, even those the culture overlooks, exploits, marginalizes, and abuses. He intentionally chooses "nobodies" to expose the hollow pretensions of the "somebodies." Everything I have—right thinking and right living, a clean slate, and a fresh start—comes from God through Jesus Christ.

I am embracing this entirely new way of life—a God-fashioned life, a life renewed from the inside out. With a new heart and a new spirit, I am empowered to follow Your commands. Your Spirit in me makes it possible for me to do what You tell me. I am filled with the power to overcome the enemy. You redeemed me, paralyzed the devil, and took the keys to death and hell. Now, the same resurrection power resides in me. Hallelujah!

Scriptures; Rom. 6:19; 1 Cor. 1:30-31; Eph 4:20-24; Luke 10:19; Is. 43:1; Rev. 1:18; Col. 2:15

A Good Name

A good name is earned by honorable behavior, godly wisdom, moral courage, and personal integrity. It is more desirable than great riches. Indeed, favor is better than silver and gold. The reward of humility is having a realistic view of my importance, and the reverent, worshipful fear of the Lord is riches, honor, and life.

I am skilled and experienced in my work. Therefore, I will stand with dignity and honor before kings and those in authority rather than stand before obscure men. For all creation is eagerly awaiting with expectation and longing earnestly for that future day when God will reveal and disclose who the sons of God, His children, really are. I am confident that I am one of them.

Prov. 22:1; Prov. 22:4; Prov. 22:29; Rom. 8:19

Who AM I

My Tongue Is The Pen Of A Ready Writer

My tongue is the pen of a ready writer. I am a wordsmith who speaks confidently about my life. I write the vision and make it plain, setting the direction, course, path, and track for my life, opening doors no man can shut. I refuse to speak negatively and close doors accidentally. My tongue will uproot, revise, reshape, renew, and reset every negative confession spoken over me or by me. My words hold the power to create a confident and constructive future.

I prophesy to myself making life-changing decrees and declarations that increase my capacity, expand my potential, and create a transformed life. My tongue will reverse every curse, every adverse circumstance, and every challenging situation. I will overcome every setback, every delay, every obstacle, every hindrance, and every obstruction on my path to destiny. What I speak will reflect the divine lineage of God that I originate from. My pedigree says:

- I am fearfully and wonderfully made (Ps. 139:14)
- I am the lender and not the borrower (Deut. 28:12)
- I am the head and not the tail (Deut. 28:12)
- I am the righteousness of God (2 Cor. 5:21)
- I am above and not beneath (Deut. 28:13)
- I am bought with a price (1 Cor. 6:20)
- I am a royal priesthood (1 Pet. 2:9)
- I am His masterpiece (Eph. 2:10)
- I have a sound mind (2 Tim 1:7)
- I am a new creation (2 Cor. 5:17)
- I am a child of God (Rom. 8:16)
- I am an overcomer (Rom. 12:21)
- I am a holy nation (1 Pet. 2:9)
- I am salt and light (Matt. 5:13-16)
- I am a conqueror (Rom. 8:37)
- I am His beloved (Col. 3:12)
- I am victorious (1 John 5:4)
- I am redeemed (Is. 43:1-2)
- I am powerful (Is. 40:29)
- I am forgiven (1 John 1:9)
- I am adopted (Eph. 1:5)
- I am faithful (Rev. 17:14)
- I am chosen (1 Pet. 2:9)
- I am strong (2 Cor. 12:10)
- I am healed (1 Pet. 2:24)
- I am whole (1 Pet. 2:24)
- I am called (Is. 43:1-2)
- I am loved (Jer. 31:3)
- I am His (IS 43:1-2)

Kingdom Jurisdiction

I am a powerful agent of change with the heart of a lion! Wherever my feet tread, I take control and dominion, asserting my influence. When I decree a thing, it becomes a reality and is established. Success is my birthright. I am a speaking spirit. When I speak, the atmosphere shifts and transforms. When I lead, I dominate and conquer every challenge. I am anointed and equipped to fight and win every battle I face. I am blessed when I enter and when I exit. Winning isn't just a habit or a goal; it's my way of life. Winning is what I do. I consistently achieve success in all that I do.

Scriptures: Deut. 11:24; Job. 22:28; Gen. 2:7; Deut. 28:6

Arise and Shine

I am the daughter of God. I am altogether beautiful. I am a darling, lovely, and beautiful in every way. The Lord delights in me, for I am more precious than any jewel—God's divine masterpiece. A crown of splendor in the Lord's hand, highly valuable in His sight. When God envisioned me, He chose to fashion me in His image and etched my name in the palm of His hand. He longs for me to dwell in His presence and drink deeply of His Spirit. For He desires to give me the Kingdom, to keep me in perfect peace, to provide me with wisdom and joy, to bring forth fruit in my life, in this season, so that whatever I do prospers. He will make me bold, strengthen, refresh, and restore my soul. Because God is within me, I WON'T FAIL! Because GOD IS WITH ME, I AM UNSTOPPABLE, IMMOVABLE, and UNTOUCHABLE! In this season, I won't look back. I will allow God to lead me. I expect signs, wonders, and miracles! God will establish the work of my hands and fulfill the promises He made to me. On this day, my path shines even brighter!

Scriptures: Prov. 4:18; Is. 40:31; John 15:5; Ps. 1; Ps. 46:5; Deut. 31:8; 2 Cor. 12:12; Ps. 90:17; 2 Cor. 1:20; Song. 5:7; Zep. 3:17; Eph. 2:10; Is. 62:3; Is. 43:4; Gen. 1:7; Is. 49:16; Ps. 27:14; Luke 12:32; Is. 26:3

Clothed With Strength

I am beautiful, highly favored, and a beloved Woman of God. Father, I am very precious. Hold me tight to Your chest, God, and keep me lifted. Make me aware of Your presence and love at all times. May Your arms always embrace me. Clothe me with strength so that I can laugh without fear of the future. Remind me that You're within me, and as a result, I will not fail. Bless me because I believe that You will fulfill Your promises to me. You have good, great, and awesome plans for my future. Fight for me so I may remain calm, strong, brave, and very courageous in the midst of the storm. Be my strength and my song before, during, and after the victory. I am altogether beautiful, beautiful in every way. A worthy woman whose price is far above rubies.

Scriptures: Ps. 118:4; Song. 4:7; Prov. 3:5; Ps. 139:14; Exo. 14:14; 2 Cor. 1:20; Jer. 29:11; Ps. 18:32; Prov. 31:25; Ps. 29:11; Ps. 46:5

Beautiful and Beloved

I am beautiful and beloved of God. I recognize the value God has placed upon my life. I am His masterpiece, fearfully and wonderfully made. I am SIGNIFICANT, PURPOSED, AND ANOINTED for this life's journey. I am seen, heard, known, and cared for by a loving God. He delights in me. My life is not an accident. I will continue to PERSEVERE over all my struggles, refusing to be intimidated by the enemy. I WILL STAY IN THE FIGHT! COMMITTED, DEVOTED, SOLID, CONSTANT, and CONSISTENT. I am well able to overcome any challenge. I qualify as a useful vessel, prepared for noble purposes. As a result, I will experience divine acceleration and decisive victories in every area of my life as I fulfill His purpose for my life.

Scriptures: Ps. 139; Eph. 2:10; Zep. 3:17; Gen. 16:11-13; Num. 13:30; 2 Tim. 2:21

I AM A Fearless Lioness

I am a beloved Daughter of God! I am His magnificent creation, the awesome and incredible handiwork of God—His DNA courses through my veins. I am designed and destined to flourish. I am a chosen vessel of God. I mount up on wings like an eagle and SOAR. Because God is with me, I experience deep, abiding joy deep down within my soul. I walk in God's divine purpose, boldness, and courage. I know that I am thoroughly empowered and equipped to fulfill my purpose as the Lord orders my footsteps. I AM BOLD. I AM COURAGEOUS. I AM STRONG. Every opposition, adversity, and situation that comes against me, God will surely deliver me. Everything God spoke comes to pass! I am not overcome with fear and insecurity. God strengthens me. God helps me and upholds me with His righteous right hand. **I AM A FEARLESS LIONESS!**

Scriptures: Is. 41:10; Gen. 1; Ps. 139; Is. 40:31; Acts 9:15; Ps. 119:133; Ps. 50:15; Is. 55:11

I AM A King, A Prophet, And A Priest

I am a man created in Your image. I am a King, a Prophet, and a Priest. Increase the anointing upon my life. Expand my territory. Increase my capacity for more. I decree and declare I will not die before my time. The enemy's assignment against my life is canceled in the name of Jesus! I will declare the works of the Lord, and with long life shall God satisfy me. I will be as bold as a lion pursuing my dreams and goals this year. I will overcome depression, distress, debt, discontentment, and discouragement. By faith, I shall recover all. Now, I will go forth, pursue, overtake, and conquer all, empowered by the Holy Spirit, fully persuaded that God will perform what He promised to me. The Lord is with me now and forevermore as I continue to be a man after God's own heart and do His will! **I AM A KING!**

Scriptures: Gen. 1:27; Chron. 4:10; Ps. 118:17

I AM A Mighty Warrior

I am God's dearly beloved Son, whom He loves. I bring Him great joy and He is well pleased with me! God honors me daily with life. My story is not over yet, and God has sent angels before me to prepare a place for me, one filled with perpetual victory because I abide in Him. God sent His word to encourage, reassure, and remind me that He has not forgotten His promises toward me. ALL of God's promises are yes and amen. He shall establish my steps. He will empower me and infuse me with increasing strength. I will experience divine strength and soar on wings like an eagle. I will run my race and not become weary; I will walk through the remainder of my life without quitting or giving up. I will sharpen my character because it's infused with purpose and destiny. I shall dwell in safety physically, emotionally, and spiritually.

God has a resting place, an oasis of peace for me. God will restore and revive my life. He will set me on the right path that leads to righteousness. He will be my strength and the chief authority in my life, and I will never have to be lonely again in my life. God will never leave me nor forsake me. There's no need to fear the future because God is with me. He is my strong tower. And I run to

Him! I will pursue Him all the days of my life, and He shall anoint my head in the presence of my enemies. I will embrace a life of integrity and heal from the inside out. God will satisfy my every desire and supercharge my life so that I can soar again. I will stand firm, stable, and enduring to the end so I can receive the Crown of Life. I am determined to live a life of unshakable confidence and integrity, and I will prosper and excel in every season. **I AM A MIGHTY WARRIOR**!!!!!

Scriptures: Ps. 147: 11-20; John 14; John 15:4; Is. 49:15; 2 Cor. 1:20; Prov. 16:9; Phil. 4:13-14; Is. 40:31; Ps. 4:8; Ps. 23:2-5; Deut. 31: 6-8; Prov. 18:10; James 1:12

I AM A Mighty Man Of God

I am a Mighty Man of God. I am anointed for greatness and significance. It is my destined portion. I am mighty among all men created in God's image. Bold, courageous, and strong. God will surely deliver me from every opposition, adversity, and situation that comes against me. Everything God has spoken will come to pass! I am never overcome with fear and insecurity, for God strengthens me. He helps me and upholds me with His righteous right hand. A refreshing wind of renewal and restoration makes me like an exceedingly great army. I am thoroughly empowered and equipped to fulfill my purpose as the Lord orders my footsteps. I impact others in a profound way. I am chosen and appointed for such a time as this! VICTORY is assuredly mine!

Scriptures: Gen. 1:27; Ps. 50:15; Ezk. 12:25; Is. 41:10; Ps. 51:12; Ezk. 37:10; Ps. 119:133; John. 15:16

I AM A Fighter

I AM SIGNIFICANT, PURPOSED, AND ANOINTED FOR THIS JOURNEY. I am seen, heard, known, and cared for by a loving God. I am legit in God's eyes, and He delights in me. My life is not an accident. I continuously PERSEVERE over all my struggles, refusing to be intimidated by the enemy. I WILL STAY IN THE FIGHT! COMMITTED, DEVOTED, SOLID, CONSTANT, and CONSISTENT. I am equipped with strength for the battle. I am well able to overcome it. For the Lord, my God, goes with me to fight for me against my enemies. He gives me the victory. The Lord renews my strength, helps me, upholds me, gives me spiritual confidence, and makes my feet like a hind's feet over all my places of responsibility. God will establish me, guard me against the evil one, and bless me with wisdom in everything I do. I decree physical, spiritual, and emotional health, and a spiritual and physical hedge of protection is placed around everything and everyone that belongs to me. God bless the work of my hands, reward my efforts, and bring me great success. God, I glorify You in all that I do!

Scriptures: Num. 13:30; Ps. 18:33; Deut. 20:4; Gen. 24:2; Is. 40:31; Hab. 3:19; 2 Thess. 3:3; Deut. 28:12; 1 Cor. 10:31

Wholeness of Body, Soul, and Mind

Health and Healing

I will not die but live and declare the works of the Lord. You are the Lord who heals me. Remove all these sicknesses and diseases from me. You set before me life and death, blessing and cursing, and I choose life. You said You love me, and because You love me, You will deliver me. When I call You, You will answer me. When I am in trouble, You will deliver me. I desire a long life and for You to show me Your salvation.

Scriptures: Ps. 118:17; Ps. 103:3; Deut. 30:19-20; Ps. 91:14-16; Is. 65:24; Ps. 50:15

Send Your Word

Father, send Your word and heal all my diseases; redeem my life from destruction. Send Your word and heal me. Father, I was born to glorify You. If I die, how will I glorify You? How will I praise You? Save me, Lord. Heal me. Bring this affliction, trouble, sickness, and disease to an utter end so this affliction shall not arise a second time. This sickness will not end in death, but rather, this sickness will bring glory to God and His son.

Scriptures: Ps. 107:20; Ps. 103:4-6; Ps. 6:5; Jer. 17:14; Nah. 1:9

Spiritual Vitality

If You can use anybody, use me mightily for Your glory, God. I am at a critical crossroads of life, and You are the chief strategist of my life. I have diligently served You all my life. I've been planted in the house of the Lord since my youth. I have flourished in Your courts. Help me to continue to grow in grace and bring forth fruit in my old age. Give me my mountain today, just like You gave Caleb.

Scriptures: Ps. 92; Josh. 14:12

Long Life

Father, I have walked in Your ways and kept Your statutes. I have followed You and obeyed You all the days of my life. Please lengthen my days on earth and give me a long, healthy life. A long life is the reward of the righteous. I believe I will live to see the goodness of the Lord in the land of the living. Lord, please fulfill the number of my days on earth.

God, You came so I can have life and life more abundantly. Your words are life and health to my flesh, and they prosper my health, life, and soul. I have a victorious voice because I speak and act upon Your word. Your word is an anchor for my soul. I call those things that be not as though they were. I have a confident expectation that something good will happen in my life. Because Your power resides in me and I am Your Beloved, I will prosper in all things and be in health, even as my soul prospers.

Father, this is the day You have made. Therefore, I choose to be glad and rejoice in it. Yes, I will be glad. You sent Your word, and Your healing power goes forth. Thank You for guiding me along the pathway of my life, advising me, and watching over me. Because my heart is the birthplace of all my increase, I chart a bold course for Your kingdom.

Scriptures: 1 Kings 3:14; Prov. 3:2; Ps. 27:13; John 10:10; Prov. 4:22; James 1:22; Heb. 6:19; Rom. 4:17; Is. 30:18; 3 John 1:2; Ps. 118:24; Ps. 107:20; Ps. 32:8; Prov. 4:23

Long Healthy Life

Long life is the reward of the righteous. Multiply my days and add years to my life. Because I have walked in Your ways, kept Your word, followed You, obeyed You as David did, please lengthen my days and give me a long, healthy life.

Scriptures: 1 Kings 3:14; Prov. 3; Prov. 16:31

Old Age

Like Moses, I desire to live to one hundred and twenty years old without my eyesight growing dim nor my natural strength abating. I will be as strong as ever. I have ears, and I will hear. I will not experience any hearing loss. I have ears that hear with crystal clarity. Because I hope in You, Lord, You renew my strength. I will soar on wings like eagles and run and not grow weary. I will walk and will not faint. My footing will be sure and firm. I will not have any balance issues that require canes or walkers. I will maintain my independence and mobility without any kind of disability. You are my safety and support. Make my feet like hinds' feet that stand firmly and make progress on the dangerous heights of testing and trouble. Set me securely upon the high places.

Scriptures: Matt. 11:25; Is. 40:31; Hab. 3:19;

Healthy Lifestyle

"According to 2 Peter 1:3, God has already given me everything I need for life and godliness." I eat right, exercise regularly, get regular screenings, get enough sleep, and focus on my dental hygiene. I exercise self-control and avoid gluttony. I remain pure and undefiled, making the necessary course corrections in my life. I cleanse myself from everything that would defile my body or spirit. I found Your words and ate them. I have tasted the goodness of

Your word. You said anyone who feeds on You will live and live forever. I put You in remembrance of Your word and decree it is so that I will live and live forever.

Scriptures: 2 Pet. 1:3; Jer. 15:16; 1 Cor. 3:17; Ps. 34:8; Prov. 4:22; Is. 43:26

Confidence Fully Rooted In God

Divinely Designed Woman

Grant me a quiet spirit and renew a steadfast spirit within me so that my beauty is not merely outward adorning or physical beauty but a beauty that flows from the inside out with a pure spirit. I am divinely designed by God in His Image and sealed with His approval—a woman after His own heart, a vessel for honor, sanctified [set apart for a special purpose and], useful to the Master, prepared for every good work. Thank You for Your transforming power within me.

Scriptures: 1 Pet. 3:4; Ps. 51:10; 1 Pet. 3; Gen. 1:27; Jn. 6:27; Acts. 13:22; 2 Tim. 2:21

Divinely Designed Man

I am divinely designed by God in His Image and sealed with His approval—a man after Your own heart, a vessel for honor, sanctified [set apart for a special purpose and], useful to You (the Master), prepared for every good work. I will not stagger at the promises of God through doubt or waver in unbelief. I am strong and empowered by faith. I desire to do Your will and give You all the glory, the honor, and the praise.

Scriptures: Gen. 1:27; John 6:27; Acts. 13:22; 2 Tim. 2:21; Rom. 4:20; Ps. 40:8; Ps. 96:8-13

Overcoming Insecurity

Because of You, I am fearfully and wonderfully made. I am a marvelous work fashioned by Your hands. You even tattooed my name on the palm of Your hand. You are always mindful of me so much that You neither slumber nor sleep. I am like clay in the potter's hands. I am a glorious vessel for Your display and honor. Continue to fashion and mold me in Your hands. I am a vessel that is sanctified and useful for the Master, prepared for every good work.

I will not focus on my physical stature or my appearance. I will not compare myself to others. But rather spend time cultivating love, joy, peace, forbearance, kindness, goodness, faithfulness, gentleness, and self-control. I celebrate others and their victories. I focus on inward characteristics that glorify God, such as self-control, wisdom, gentleness, fairness, impartiality, devoutness, and respect. I desire to do the will of God in every area of my life. I cast all negative imaginations down and walk away from those who fuel insecurities. I am as bold as a lion. I refuse to focus on my inadequacies because, as You are, so am I. When I look in the mirror, I see that I am a reflection of You. The DNA of Christ is in my blood.

Scriptures: Ps. 139:14; Ps. 8:4-9; Is. 49:16; Ps. 121:2-4; Jer. 18:6; 2 Tim. 2:20-21; Job 10:8; Gal. 5:22-24;

Mark 3:33-35; 2 Cor. 10:5; Prov. 28:1; 1 John 4:17; Gen. 1:27

Confidence in My Physical Appearance

Father, You said I am altogether beautiful, and because I am created in Your image, there is no flaw in me. I have a lovely figure. I am kindhearted, for I am fearfully and wonderfully made, Your wonderful handiwork. I am clothed in strength and dignity. Father, I pray that others will not only look at my outward appearance but at my heart as well. Let my spirit and light shine from the inside out and glorify my Creator.

Scriptures: Ps. 139:14; Gen. 1:27; Eph. 2:10; Prov. 31:25; Matt. 5:16

Children Are A Gift From God

When Desiring A Baby

Children are a heritage from the Lord, and the fruit of the womb is His reward. You said the barren woman will keep house and be a joyful mother of children. According to Deuteronomy 28:11, You, Lord, desire to bless me with many children. Thank you that my spouse has high-quality sperm and a large sperm count. Your name is greater than polycystic ovarian syndrome (PCOS), hypothalamic dysfunction, primary ovarian insufficiency, excessive prolactin, and other causes of infertility.

Father, You said there will be no miscarriages or infertility in the land. Therefore, without any hindrances or blockages, the egg must release from the ovaries, attach to the sperm, become fertilized, travel through the fallopian tube, and attach inside the uterus. The seed will take root firmly in my womb, and I will conceive. My body's immune system will not reject or attack my baby.

I bind all genetic disorders and RH incompatibility. I bind any stillbirths and other complications during this pregnancy. The labor and delivery staff, the mother/baby staff, and specialists are thoroughly equipped, competent, and knowledgeable experts to handle my situation. The baby will be full-term and will also have no complications during delivery. This child will fulfill its number of days on the earth. We bind the spirit of anxiety and a lack of peace because no good thing will You withhold from those who walk uprightly.

Scriptures: Ps. 127:3; Ps. 113:9; Deut. 28:11

Overcoming Barrenness

Like Sarah, there's no deadness in my womb. By faith, I receive strength to conceive seed and will deliver a child when I am past age because You are faithful who promised. Jesus, You are the same yesterday, today, and forever. Therefore, I will bring forth a child. I am confident that if I ask anything according to Your will, You will hear me. And because I know that You hear me, whatsoever I ask, I know that I have received the petitions of my heart that I desire from You.

Scriptures: Heb. 11:11; 1 John 5:14-15

Desire for Children

God, remember me like You remembered Hannah and make it possible for me to have children. Please allow me to live and not die in childbirth so that I may live a full life and die at a good, ample, and full age. Satisfied and satiated, where my eyes are not dim, nor my natural force abated, and my memory intact.

God, my heart exalts and triumphs in You. My Horn, my strength, is lifted up in the Lord. There is no one Holy like You. There is none besides You. There is no rock like my God. Remember me when my husband knows me intimately, and may the child be filled with the Holy Spirit from the womb. My soul magnifies and extols You, Lord. And my spirit rejoices in God, my Savior. That all may be fulfilled as You've spoken and shown me.

Scriptures: 1 Sam 1:19; Job 5:26; Deut. 34:7; 1 Sam. 2:1-3; Jer. 10:6; Luke 1:41; Luke 1:4-6

Fruitfulness

Father, I pray there will be no miscarriages, barrenness, or infertility in the land because I am Your beloved. You desire that I prosper in all things and be in health, just as my soul prospers. Therefore, help me to bear fruit and be fruitful in my womb.

Scriptures: Exo. 23:26; 3 John 1:2; John 15:8

Raising Godly Children

My child/children are a gift from the Lord. They are a reward from Him. Jesus loves children and desires that they all come to Him because the kingdom of heaven belongs to them. I will guide my children in the right direction because God promises that they will not depart from it even when they are old. I endeavor to sit and study with my children at home, and when we are out and about, when we lie down, and when we get up

I have no greater joy than hearing that my children are walking in the truth of God's word. I will not irritate or anger them, causing them to turn away from me or God. I will discipline them wisely and not spare the rod because I love them. God guarantees that I will enjoy peace and experience wonderful rewards that delight my heart.

God loves that my children's hearts are moved to worship Him, and they keep all His commandments because they love Him. I have spent time training and teaching them about my great God. When we engage in worshipping, studying, and meditating on the Word, these behaviors lead to and confirm that all will go well with me and my children forever! My children will be my crown in my old age.

Scriptures: Ps. 127:13; Matt. 19:14; Prov. 22:16; Deut. 6:6-9; 3 John 1:4; Col. 3:21; Prov. 13:24; Ps. 37; Eph. 6:1-4; Prov. 17:6

Prayer for Prodigal Children

My prodigal (son/daughter) will return home. Father, You said that when I train up my child in the Word, in the way they should go, they won't depart from it when they are old. One day, my child will glorify You and come home. Father, my child is a gift from You. Before You formed them in the womb, You knew them, consecrated them, and appointed them a prophet to the nation. They are called of You. My child will become a leader in Your church.

Send individuals across his/her path to minister the Word of God to them. You love my child, and I ask You to bring them back home. Father, You said I would behold and see the new thing You would do in my child's life. I pray that the Holy Spirit will work and transform their life. Because the devil comes only to steal and kill and destroy, the devil can't have my daughter/son. I pray for a hedge of protection around them. Dispatch Your angels to the north, south, west, and east to guard them and send their enemies away in terror.

Scriptures: Prov.22:6; Ps.127: 3; Jer.1:5; Is. 43:19; John 10:10; Exo. 23:20-33

Prayers/Declarations for An Ill Child

Father, I declare all is well. Save my child, please. One word from You can change my life and change my circumstances. This situation is not dead. O Lord my God, please let my child's spirit return to his body. Revive my child! Lord, You are the God who hears and answers prayers. Let my child's life return to their body and be revived, and I will declare that my child lives because You, Lord, are good, faithful, and merciful.

Father, You have all authority over sin and death. I won't be afraid. I will not doubt it. I will not allow unbelief and disbelief in my presence. I will only believe that You will heal my child. I desire to see the glory of God manifest in my child's life. Jesus, this is my only child. Let Your heart overflow with compassion because I place my faith in You. Command my child to get up and give my child back to me. You possess all power and can make my child whole and live again.

Scriptures: 2 Kings 4:26; Is. 55:11; 2 Kings 4:34; 1 John 5:14-15; 1 Cor. 15:57; Acts 9:40; Mark 5:36; Mark 5:21-43

Family Confessions

Family Treaty

A house divided against itself cannot stand. Therefore, as for me and my house, we will serve the Lord. God has chosen my family as his own special people. We belong to him, and he loves us very much. We are kind to each other. We help each other. We respect each other and exercise patience with one another. When we become angry, we will not remain angry or let the sun go down on our anger. We forgive quickly because the Lord has forgiven us.

Scriptures: Mark 3:25; Jos. 24:15; Ps. 33:12; 1 Cor. 3: 22-23; Col 3:13-17

God-Fearing Family

Love is patient; love is kind. It does not envy, boast, or demonstrate pride. It does not dishonor others, is not self-seeking, is not easily angered, and keeps no record of wrongs. Love does not delight in evil but rejoices with the truth. It always protects, always trusts, always hopes, always perseveres in our household. Christ is the head. The head of every man is Christ, and the head of the woman is man. Mutual submission exists between husband and wife. Love and mutual respect are fixtures in our family. It is the foundation for how we manage our household. Our children are obedient and not rebellious. They are a blessing and a precious gift. We nurture and raise them in the ways of the Lord.

We are a God-fearing family dedicated to giving generously to advance the kingdom. We honor God with our first fruits, the tithe, and the offering. We pray regularly to God and maintain our fellowship with Him. We are unwavering in our commitment to God. We bear with each other, forgiving one another. Where there are grievances, we forgive as God forgave us. We are committed to family unity and do not allow strife to become a stronghold. Our family is a blessing to others. Our family serves others. Bless our house, and we will multiply, prosper, and increase as You commanded. Lord, bless our home.

Scriptures: 1 Cor. 13:4-7; 1 Cor. 11:3; Acts 10:2; 1 Tim 3:4; Col 3:13

Unity in the Family

My family and I operate in a spirit of oneness, togetherness, and harmony. We imitate the unity that exists between God, Jesus, and the Holy Spirit. They operate with a spirit of oneness. We are like-minded, sharing the same love, and we are unified in spirit and purpose. The Word of God serves as the standard in our home. We tie them to our hands and wear them on our foreheads as reminders. We write them on the doorposts of our house and on our gates.

We make every effort to keep the unity of the Spirit through the bond of peace. We each possess different gifts that allow us to function in one accord and agreement. This coordination leads to perfect unity. We are peacemakers, striving to live in peace with one another. Because we are like Christ, we forgive each other often. We won't give the devil a place in our homes or our hearts. The devil can't have anything that belongs to my family. We submit to the Word of God and resist the devil, causing him to flee. Because we fight the good fight of faith, our family always wins.

Scriptures: Eph. 4:5; Deut. 6:6-8; Eph. 4:3; 1 Cor. 12:12-26; Rom. 12:18; James 4:7; 1 Tim. 6:12

Children

My precious children are a heritage from the LORD and a true reward from Him. They are like arrows in my hands, and I am dedicated to guiding them along the righteous path. I am truly blessed because my quiver is full. I teach them to honor their parents so they may live long in the land of the LORD. I teach my children to obey me in everything, for this pleases the Lord and brings joy to His heart. I will not frustrate my children; instead, I will bring them up in the training and instruction of the Lord.

I train my children in the way they should go, and even when they are old, they will not turn from it. I impress Your commandments upon my children. I discuss Your commandments when we sit at home, walk along the road, lie down, and get up. This is so that my children will thrive and prosper in the land the LORD my God has destined for them.

Scriptures: Deut. 5:6; Exo 20:12; Prov 22:6; Col 3:20; Ps 127:3-5; Eph 6:1-2

Young King Confession

Young King, you are no ordinary child! You are a unique and special royal heir destined for greatness! You will have divine encounters with God, and He will pour out His spirit upon you, and you shall prophesy. Expect the manifestation of God's power in your life. You have come to the kingdom for such a time as this. You are indeed God's masterpiece, chosen and ordained before you were formed in your mother's womb.

I decree and declare that blessings shall overtake you all the days of your life, and with long life shall God satisfy you. He gives His angels charge over you to protect you in everything you do. May you delight in the Lord all the days of your life and imitate Him in all your ways. May the joy of the Lord be your strength.

May you grow in wisdom, in stature, and in favor with God and man. I bind every plot, every scheme, every plan of the devil. They shall not prosper against you.

And one day, you shall marry a woman who loves the Lord as much as you, and your healthy union shall glorify the Lord.

Remain strong and courageous, knowing the Lord designed you to succeed in life, and He will never leave, forsake, or abandon you. Blessings Always!

Scriptures: 1 Pet. 2:9; Joel 2:28-32; Acts 2:15-21; Esther 4:14; Eph. 2:10; Jer. 1:5; Deut. 28:2; Ps. 91:16; Ps. 91:11; Ps. 37:4; Eph. 5:1; Neh. 8:10; Luke 2:52; Is. 54:17; Deut. 31:6; Jos. 1:9

Beloved Daughter Confession

Beloved Daughter, you are no ordinary child! You are a unique and special royal heir, destined for greatness! You will have divine encounters with God, and He will pour out His spirit upon you, and you shall prophesy. Expect the manifestation of God's power in your life. You have come to the kingdom for such a time as this. You are indeed God's masterpiece, chosen and ordained before you were formed in your mother's womb.

I decree and declare that blessings shall overtake you all the days of your life, and with long life shall God satisfy you. He gives His angels charge over you to protect you in everything you do. May you delight in the Lord all the days of your life and imitate Him in all your ways. May the joy of the Lord be Your strength.

May you grow in wisdom, in stature, and in favor with God and man. I bind every plot, every scheme, every plan of the devil. They shall not prosper against you. And one day, you shall marry a man who loves the Lord as much as you, and your healthy union shall glorify the Lord.

Remain strong and courageous, knowing the Lord designed you to succeed in life, and He will never leave, forsake, or abandon you. Blessings Always!

Scriptures: 1 Pet. 2:9; Joel 2:28-32; Acts 2:15-21; Esther 4:14; Eph. 2:10; Jer. 1:5; Deut. 28:2; Ps. 91:16; Ps. 91:11; Ps. 37:4; Eph. 5:1; Neh. 8:10; Luke 2:52; Is. 54:17; Deut. 31:6; Jos. 1:9

Love Never Fails

Love

If you love me, you will keep my commandments. Love never fails. It binds everything together in perfect harmony. Love is very patient and kind, never jealous or envious, never boastful or proud, never haughty or selfish or rude. Love does not demand its own way. It is not irritable or touchy. Love does not hold grudges and will hardly even notice when others do it wrong. It is never glad about injustice, but rejoices whenever truth prevails. When I love someone, I am loyal to them, no matter the cost. I will always believe in them, always expect the best of them, and always stand my ground in defending them. I let all that I do be done in love.

Scriptures: John 14:15; 1 Cor. 13

A Woman Desiring Marriage

I will not be anxious about anything, but in everything, by prayer and supplication with thanksgiving, I let my requests be made known to God. Every good and perfect gift is from above, coming down from the Father of the heavenly lights, who does not change like shifting shadows. Your timing, Father, is perfect, and I will not be impatient and take matters into my own hands regarding my desire to marry. Just like Boaz noticed Ruth, so shall my future husband notice me as I serve in the house of the Lord.

Two are better than one because they have a good return for their labor: If either of them falls down, one can help the other up. I will not be yoked together or fellowship with unbelievers. The righteous and wicked have nothing in common nor light with darkness. You set the lonely in families. Lord, grant my petition, which I have asked of You, for a husband who will love me like Isaac loved Rebecca, Jacob loved Rachel, Elkanah loved Hannah, and Boaz loved Ruth.

Scriptures: Phil 4:6; James 1:17; Ps. 37:34; Ruth 2; Ecc. 4:9-10; 2 Cor. 6:14; Ps. 56:5; Gen. 24:67; Gen. 29:18; 1 Sam. 1:4; Ruth 1-4

True Love

I have found the one whom my soul loves. He/she nourishes my soul. The fruit of the Spirit, love, joy, peace, patience, gentleness, goodness, faith, meekness, and self-control reign supreme in my potential mate. We live in the Spirit and walk in the Spirit. We operate with understanding, and we exercise control of our anger. We do not have a hot temper or operate foolishly. We do not worry about anything. Instead, we pray about everything that results in great peace that guards our hearts and minds. There's no selfish ambition in our hearts; therefore, we are not bitterly jealous. The joy of the Lord is our strength.

Scriptures: Song. 3:4; Gal. 5:22-25; Prov. 14:29; Phil 4:6-7; Neh. 8:10

A Woman Desiring A Mate

Lord, help me to be a suitable helpmate. Lord, make me very beautiful, attractive, chaste, and modest—a woman of strength, worth, bravery, and capability. My husband will love me like Jacob loved Rachel, who was more beautiful and attractive than any other woman. Give me uncommon wisdom to handle the affairs of our home and enrich my husband's life. Furthermore, let my husband treat me like Boaz treated Ruth and make provisions for me.

Make my house like the house of Perez, whom Tamar bore to Judah, because of the offspring that the Lord will give my husband for me. Lord, cause me to conceive and bear a son, bear twins. Give me double for my trouble, restoration, and redemption. Lord, make me like Rachel and Leah, who built the household of Israel. May my husband do it worthily and get wealth and power.

Scriptures: Gen. 29:18; Gen. 2:18; Gen. 24:16; Ruth 3:11; Prov. 31; Ruth 4:12; Is. 61:7; Ruth 4:11

Desiring Marriage/Sexual Purity

Father, You said it's not good for man to be alone and that two are better than one. Father, I pray that You will send a suitable helpmate, one designed just for me. I pray that as I serve in the house of the Lord, he/she will notice me. I pray that we will have compatibility in many areas that bring victory to Your kingdom and many others. This courtship and marriage will glorify You.

Inappropriate interactions, touching, heavy breathing, petting, fornication, masturbation, and pornography shall not be named among us. Family and marriage are Your ideas, Lord. I choose right and notice the red flags that have the potential to harm our courtship and future together. Help us to do the work that fosters healing, prevents future conflicts, and promotes harmony and peace in our home and our relationship.

Scriptures: Gen. 2:18; 1 Cor. 16:18

A Man Desiring Marriage

It is not good for a man to be alone. God will make a helper fit for me. I will find a wife because this is a good thing, and I will obtain favor from the LORD. It is the will of God that I abstain from sexual immorality before marriage. I will control my body and maintain holiness and honor. I will not engage in passion or lust. Charm is deceptive, and beauty is fleeting, but a woman who fears the Lord is to be praised. She will love the Lord her God with all her heart, with all her soul, and with all her mind. Once I am married, I will leave my father and mother, hold fast to my wife, and we will become one flesh.

Scriptures: Prov. 18:22; 1 Cor. 16; Prov. 31:30; Matt. 22:27; Matt. 19:5

God's Design For Marriage

The Pillars of Marriage

I have found the one whom my soul loves. We encourage and build each other up. May the Lord increase and overflow our love for each other. We are devoted to each other in love, honoring one another more than we honor ourselves. My spouse's joy matters deeply to me. I commit to being emotionally available by dedicating quality time to my spouse, fully engaged while sharing my thoughts, emotions, and vulnerabilities openly and without reservation. I also commit to becoming a good listener by not interrupting, responding with empathy, and striving to understand my spouse's perspective. This is my heartfelt commitment to my spouse: to always be there for them, to love and support them in every endeavor they pursue.

Let us be sensitive and attuned to each other's needs, wants, and desires. Deepening, strengthening, and increasing our connection and bond so we remain in sync and in perfect harmony. One person standing alone can be attacked and defeated, but two can stand back-to-back and conquer. Three are even better, for a triple-braided cord is not quickly broken. Send us mentors who will equip, empower, and provide insight to help us grow and mature into better marital partners. We aim to glorify God with our marriage by living out the values and principles of love, respect, and faithfulness, and by serving as an example to others of a union blessed by God for a divine purpose.

Faith, hope, and love remain. But the greatest of these is love: "Love is patient, love is kind. It does not envy, it does not boast, it is not proud. It does not dishonor others. It is not self-seeking. It is not easily angered, and it keeps no record of wrongs. Love does not delight in evil but rejoices with the truth. It always protects, always trusts, always hopes, always perseveres. I commit to unwavering faithfulness, to keeping our marriage bed undefiled by avoiding adultery and pornography. I commit to being a cheerful giver to my spouse because my gift of generosity will return to me in full with overflowing measure, pressed down, shaken together, making room for more, and running over. This is my commitment to you, to our marriage, and to our future together.

Scriptures: 1 Cor. 13; 1 Cor. 13:13; Heb. 13:4; Song. 3:4; 1 Thess. 5:11; 1 Thess. 3:12; Rom. 12:10; Ecc. 4:12; Luke 6:38

Covenant Love

I am my beloved's, and my beloved is mine. Don't urge me to leave you or to turn back from you. Where you go, I will go, and where you stay, I will stay. Your people will be my people and your God my God. Where you die, I will die, and there I will be buried. May the Lord deal with me, be it ever so severely, if even death separates you and me.

We are one flesh. Therefore, what God joined together, no one will separate. We love each other deeply, and our love covers a multitude of sins. We are kind and compassionate to one another, forgiving each other, just as Christ forgave us. God has joined us together. We are unified in spirit, and no one can separate us.

Scriptures: Song. 3:3; Ruth 1:16; Gen. 2:24; Matt. 19:6; 1 Pet. 4:8; Eph. 4:32; Eph. 4:3

Walking in Love

Father, I love You because You first loved me. I am an imitator of God, my Heavenly Father. I copy Him and follow His example because I am His well-beloved child. I imitate Him by walking in love, esteeming and delighting in others as Christ loved us and gave Himself up for us. I let my love be sincere, a real thing. I hate what is evil and loathe all ungodliness. I turn in horror from wickedness, but hold fast to that which is good.

I love others with brotherly affection, treating them as family members and showing them preferential treatment and honor. You said that no one has greater love or shown stronger affection than to lay down their life for their friends. I put on, then, as God's chosen one, a compassionate heart, kindness, humility, meekness, and patience, bearing with one another, and if one has a complaint against another, forgiving each other as the Lord has forgiven me. Above all, I put on love which binds everything together in perfect harmony, letting all that I do be done in love.

Scriptures: John 15:13; John 4:18; 1 John 4:19; Rom. 18:9-10; Col. 3:12-14.; 1 Cor. 16:14

Forgiveness

Father, thank you for Your mercy toward me. You have not dealt with me according to my sins or repaid me according to my iniquities. You removed my transgressions from me as far as the East is from the West. You blotted out my transgressions, washed me thoroughly from my iniquity, and cleansed me from my sin. I am blessed because my transgressions are forgiven, and my sin is covered. I am blessed because there's no iniquity or deceit in my spirit. I pray and confess my sins to You often, confidently knowing that You will forgive my iniquity. As You forgave me, I commit to forgive anyone who wrongs or sins against me seventy times seven. You are a comforting hiding place for me; You preserve me from trouble; You surround me with shouts of deliverance, filling me with a deep sense of security and reassurance.

Scriptures: Ps. 103:10-12; Ps. 51:1-2; Ps. 32:1-7; Matt. 18:21-22

Overcoming Sickness and Disease

Arthritis

Father, I put You in remembrance of Your word. You said that You would bring health and healing. I listen carefully to Your teaching and to everything that You tell me. I will never forget Your words. I keep them upon my tongue, my mind, and my heart. Your Word gives true life to anyone who takes hold of it. It will give health to my whole body, remove any trace of sickness and disease, and destroy the works of the devil.

Bring health and healing to the pain in my joints and body. I bind the symptoms of arthritis, osteoarthritis, temporal arthritis, psoriatic arthritis, and gout, which manifest with pain, stiffness, warm sensations, joint swelling, redness, and inflammation. Please help me run and not be weary; walk and not faint. Please help me not to become addicted to pain medications, but rather rely on You for the full manifestation of my healing. Have mercy on me, Lord, for I am faint. Heal me, Lord, for my bones are in agony. Strengthen me and help me with Your righteous right hand.

Scriptures: Is. 43:26; Jer. 33:6; Prov. 4:20-22; Is. 40:29-31; Ps. 6:2; Is. 41:10; Prov. 3:8; I John 3:8

Alzheimer's and Dementia

I have a sound mind. My mind is renewed daily by the word of God. I gird up the loins of my mind by being mentally alert and prepared for action. My head is in the game. I enjoy and live a very healthy lifestyle. My body is the temple of God, and therefore, I avoid all illicit activities such as drinking, smoking, and drugs. I exercise and eat right. Alzheimer's and Dementia may be in my family bloodline and lineage, but it stopped with them. Alzheimer's and Dementia are not a part of my destiny. It is not in my DNA.

I have the mind of Christ. He does not forget me, nor shall I forget my children or any of my memories. I can recall things instantly, like where I parked my car, any assignments for school or work, phone numbers, and the names of family, friends, coworkers, associates, and acquaintances. I do not misplace things easily. I pay my bills and handle my money with ease. I know where I am going at all times. I don't keep repeating the same thing or experience changes in my mood, personality, or behavior. I master technology easily.

I am the servant of the Lord. He formed me and will not forget me. The Lord thinks about me constantly. He has numerous thoughts about me, and when I awaken in the morning, He's still thinking about me. I will not be afraid or discouraged because the Lord has already gone ahead of me personally. The Lord will be with me, and

He will neither fail nor abandon me. Just like the Lord remembers everything, so will I! The memory of the righteous is blessed, and the Lord will perfect that which concerns me.

Scriptures: 2 Tim 1:7; Rom 12:2; 1 Pet. 1:13; 1 Cor. 6:19-20; 1 Cor. 2:16; Is. 49:15

Brain Fog

For God is not a God of confusion but of peace. I am created in His image; therefore, I don't experience confusion, forgetfulness, difficulty paying attention, concentrating, or losing my train of thought. God, please place the right words in my mouth and allow the Holy Spirit to teach me what to say at the right time so I can react quickly to whatever is occurring and have the right words to say. Your words are active, effective, and powerful, producing the intended result. The Helper, the Holy Spirit, teaches me all things and brings back to my remembrance all that has been said when I lose my train of thought. The Word of God is at work in me because I believe. It is vibrant, dynamic, energizing, and productive; as a result, I won't experience mental exhaustion or fatigue. I prepare my mind for action, being alert, focused, and self-controlled. I vigilantly dwell on my manifested healing. I am renewed in the spirit of my mind, and it permeates my heart, soul, and mind.

Scriptures: 1 Cor. 14:33; Luke 12:11-12; 1 Thess. 2:13; John 14:26; Eph. 4:3; 1 Pet. 1:13

Fighting Cancer

I refuse to die because You are the Resurrection and the Life. The Zoe life of Christ flows through my veins. I will live and not die and declare the works of the Lord. I speak to cancer and its uncontrolled cell growth and tumor formation and command it to cease in the name of Jesus. I speak to the root of every inherited genetic mutation and command it to cease its rapid and repeated production in the name of Jesus. The DNA of Christ, the DNA repair gene, will proliferate in my body and regulate healthy cell growth. This is my covenant right. Bring health to my body and nourishment to my bones. Multiply my days and add years to my life.

Scriptures: John 11:25-26; Ps. 118:17; Prov. 3:8; Prov. 9:11-12

Healing from Diseases

Father, I put You in remembrance of Your word. You said, "That You would bring health and healing. I listen carefully to Your teachings and to everything that You tell me. I will never forget Your words. I keep them upon my tongue, my mind, and my heart. Your Word gives true life to anyone who takes hold of it. It will give health to my whole body, remove any trace of sickness and disease, and destroy the works of the devil.

Lord, forgive all of my sins and heal all my diseases:

A

aneurysm, **pancreatitis,** Addison's disease, allergies, Alzheimer's disease, angina, all types of cancer, all eating disorders, anorexia nervosa, angioedema, ankylosing spondylitis, appendicitis, asthma, all autistic spectrum disorders, attention deficit hyperactivity disorder, atrial fibrillation, abscesses, anxiety,

B

Bulimia, Blindness, blood clots, benign prostate enlargement, binge eating, sepsis, gut issues, bowel incontinence, brain stem death, bronchitis, bunions,

C

Cellulitis, cerebral palsy, chest pain, Cholecystitis, chronic fatigue syndrome, chronic kidney disease, COPD, pancreatitis, cirrhosis, C-diff, Celiac disease, congenital heart disease, conjunctivitis, constipation, Covid-19, Crohn's disease, cystic fibrosis, cystitis, croup, cysts of all kinds,

D

Deafness, DVT, dehydration, depression, dementia, diabetes, diverticulitis, dizziness, swallowing problems, dystonia, diarrhea, Down's syndrome, all forms of diabetes,

E

Ebola, ectopic pregnancy, ear infection, endometriosis, epilepsy, erectile dysfunction, E. coli, eczema, and all skin disorders,

F

Fatty liver disease, Fibroids, fibromyalgia, food poisoning, fungal nail infections,

G

Gallstones, ganglion cysts, gastroenteritis, GERD, gout, gum disease,

H

Hemorrhoids, hearing loss, hay fever, heart failure, heart attacks, Hepatitis A, B, and C, hernias, high cholesterol, hives, HIV - AIDs, Hodgkin Lymphomas, Huntington's disease, hyperglycemia (high blood sugar), hypoglycemia (low blood sugar),

K

Kidney stones, kidney infections,

L

Lactose intolerance, laryngitis, leg cramps, leukemia, lice, liver diseases, lymphoedema, labyrinthitis, lupus, Lyme disease,

M

Malaria, malnutrition, measles, meningitis, menopause, painful menstrual cramps, mesothelioma, ear infections, migraines, miscarriages, mumps, Meniere's disease, Myasthenia gravis,

N

Neuroblastoma, Non-Hodgkin Lymphoma, norovirus, nosebleeds,

O

Obesity, obsessive-compulsive disorder (OCD), osteoporosis, osteosarcoma, obstructive sleep apnea, overactive thyroid,

P

Paget's disease, panic disorder, Parkinson's disease, pelvic inflammatory disease, prolapses of all kinds, peripheral neuropathy, personality disorders, pleurisy, pneumonia, polycystic ovary syndrome, post-traumatic stress disorder (PTSD), postnatal depression, pressure ulcers, psoriasis, psychosis,

R

Raynaud's phenomenon, restless legs syndrome, ringworm, rosacea,

S

Scabies, scarlet fever, schizophrenia, scoliosis, all sexually transmitted diseases, shortness of breath, shingles, sickle cell disease, sinusitis, Sjogren's syndrome, skin cancer all types, skin rashes, sore throat, stillbirth, stress, low mood, sudden infant death syndrome (SIDS), suicide, all forms of sarcoma, seizures, streptococcus, sunburn, supraventricular tachycardia, strokes, swollen glands,

T

Thrush, All testicular issues, threadworms, tinnitus, tonsillitis, toothaches and decay, TIA, trigeminal neuralgia, TB, transverse myelitis,

U

All kinds of ulcers, ulcerative colitis, underactive thyroid, urinary incontinence, UTI,

V

Vaginal discharges, vitamin B12 deficiency, vertigo,

W

Warts, whooping cough, Wilms tumor, and

Y

Yellow fever.

Scriptures: Is. 43:26; Jer. 33:6; Prov. 4:20-22; Prov. 3:8; 1 John 3:8; Ps. 103:3

Distress

Father, I cry out to You. Please save me from my distress. Free me from my suffering. Rescue me from the grave. Take away the sickness from my midst because I worship You, Lord. I live a victorious life because You bore my pain and suffering.

Scriptures: Ps. 18:6; Ps. 25:17; Exo. 28:25; Is. 53:4

Complete Recovery from All Types of Cancer

Father, I pray for all types of cancer (brain, breast, bladder, colon, endometrial, head and neck cancer, lung, ovarian, pancreatic, skin, thyroid, etc.), and thank You for Your healing power. We bind the spirit of fear and loose the spirit of peace, for You are my Light and my Salvation. Whom shall I fear or dread? For You are my refuge and my stronghold. Of whom shall I be afraid? Bring life and not death. Allow healing to manifest quickly and minimize all side effects of chemotherapy and radiation, vomiting, and dehydration. Strengthen me. Sustain me upon my sickbed and restore my health, help me up from this bed of illness, rescue me from the grave, and let me live a long life.

Scriptures: Ps. 27:1; Ps. 91:2; Ps. 41:1-3

Quicken My Mortal Body

Renew my youth, O Lord, as I humbly submit myself in obedience to Your word. The fear of the Lord, a deep reverence and awe for Your power and authority, is the source of my life. I have a sound and peaceful heart, free from jealousy and envy. My heart gives life and revitalizes my body. Grant me renewed strength and sustained physical and mental health in my old age. Infuse and quicken my mortal body with Your Spirit so I may enjoy good, robust health. Restore my life. As I wait upon the Lord, You will renew my strength, enabling me to soar like an eagle, run tirelessly, and walk without growing weary.

Scripture: Prov 14:27, 30; Is. 40:31

Physical, Mental, and Spiritual Disciplines

My body is the temple of the Holy Spirit. Therefore, I honor God with my body. I exercise self-control in all areas of my life, from uncontrolled appetites, ungodliness, and worldly passions that lead to disease, slow death, and destruction. Mental and physical health is like wealth to my soul and an asset to me. Because I am Your Beloved, You desire that I succeed, prosper, and be physically healthy, just as my soul prospers spiritually. Help me to be healthy physically and emotionally so I can carry the anointing of God.

Therefore, to succeed, prosper, and maintain good health, I exercise for at least 30 minutes a day, knowing that it improves my mood and strengthens my physical body. I eat healthily because it provides my body with the fuel and energy it needs to fight sickness and disease. My diet consists of fish, grapes, figs, pomegranates, various fruits, vegetables, whole grains, protein-rich foods, almonds, peanuts, and other foods as recommended by my doctor. Water is a source of blessing, renewal, cleansing, healing, and life. As a result, water is a staple in my diet. No alcohol, smoking, or sexually improper activities will be a part of my life. I desire to please You in the way that I live. I remove all ungodliness and worldly passions and live a self-controlled, upright, and godly life,

Father, You grant sweet sleep to those whom You love. This sweet, good-quality sleep is essential to repairing my body, mood, thoughts, and memory. It improves my body's performance, function, and reliability. Physical exercise carries great value. Therefore, I commit to exercising daily for at least 30 minutes. Walking is important to You, as You mention it over 300 times in the Bible. Consequently, this is my preferred method of maintaining a healthy weight.

Help me develop the discipline to engage in physical fitness, which in turn helps with mental clarity. I take captive every thought, over every mental stronghold, depression, feelings of resentment, worthlessness, trauma, pain, shame, guilt, disappointments, and regret. I pull down strongholds and imaginations. I fix my thoughts on what is true, honorable, right, pure, lovely, and admirable, and that brings peace. I reflect on these things by meditating on what is excellent and worthy of praise.

Lastly, I engage in spiritual exercises of meditation, prayer, worship, and reading my Word, which reinforces my kingdom identity and authority. I call to You, God, because healing is in Your wings. Answer me and show me great and mighty things. Heal my mental and physical wounds as I put on this new man by renewing my mind and body daily. These physical, mental, and spiritual goals increase my life expectancy and improve my overall health. Bring health and healing to me so I can enjoy abundant shalom and security and receive that eventual everlasting crown of life.

Scriptures; 1 Cor. 6:19-20; Lev 11:9; Eph. 4:22-23; Jer 33:6; I Tim 4:8-10; 2 Cor 10:4-5; 3 John 1:2; Jer. 33:6; Tit. 2:11-12; Phil. 4:8

Headaches/Migraines

Father, the head represents authority, honor, and responsibility. Yet, I am currently challenged, afflicted, and burdened relentlessly with tension headaches, cluster headaches, sinus headaches, and migraines, which causes me to experience dizziness, fatigue, nausea, visual disturbances, vomiting, and sensitivity to light, sound, or smells. The frequency, severity, and duration of these headaches and migraines are debilitating and present significant barriers that prevent me from participating in activities, working, and taking care of my family. I am tired and weary of relying on over-the-counter medications and constantly avoiding specific triggers. Through it all, I hold on to my faith with confidence. You are the lifter of my head, Lord. Heal me, LORD, and I will be healed, for blessings crown the head of the righteous.

Scriptures: Ps. 3:3; Jer. 17:4; Prov. 10:6

Recovering From A Stroke

When stroke-like symptoms such as facial drooping, weakness or numbness in my arm or leg on one side, slurred speech or difficulty speaking, confusion, difficulty in seeing, dizziness, loss of balance or coordination, and a severe headache present, I remember Your words, "Don't be afraid, for I am with You. Don't be discouraged, for I am Your God." You will strengthen, help, and uphold me with Your victorious right hand."

Lord, my God, I call upon You for help, and You hear and heal me. It is impossible with man, but not with You, God, for with You, God, all things are possible. My recovery journey will be an incredible miracle. I place my request before You for healing, and the prayer offered in faith will make the sick person well, and You will raise me up.

I will arise and walk, regaining mobility in my limbs because You have forgiven my sins. I possess muscle memory, and my muscles will continue to receive signals from the brain and move. Restore any contractures or withered hands like You did for King Jeroboam when the prophet prayed for him and the man You healed on the Sabbath. Please do the same for me, Lord, so I can work and be a productive and profitable citizen.

Address this foot drop that prevents me from lifting my toes, causes me to trip, and makes it difficult for me to walk. Mark out a straight path for my feet so that even though I am weak and lame, I will not fall, but become strong.

And just as You blessed Eliezer so he could swallow water with ease, allow me to overcome my swallowing difficulties. Lord, I also suffer from a speech impairment, slurred speech, or aphasia. You said, "*Ephatha*," which means "be opened," to the deaf man with a speech impediment, and his tongue was loosened, allowing him to speak plainly.

You always hear me when I pray. I exercise the gift of faith. I ask You to do all this for me, Lord, and I will return and wholeheartedly express my gratitude and worship You with all my heart, soul, and mind. Bring wholeness back to my life, Lord, physically, mentally, emotionally, and spiritually. Manifest Your glorious healing power in my life.

Scripture: Matt 9:1-8; Ps. 30:2; James 5:15; Mark 10:27; Matt. 12: 9-14; Heb. 12:13; Gen. 24:17; 1 John 5:14-15; Luke 17:11-19

Victory Over Stress-Related Fatigue

Lord, I acknowledge that You give power to the faint and to the individual with no might, You increase strength. The stress of work, challenges at home, and unsettling global events significantly affect my performance and overall well-being, leading to chronic persistent stress. Despite all of my self-care attempts, I remain worn out, drained, and exhausted, which impacts my enthusiasm, motivation, disposition, quality of life, well-being, and happiness. I ask for Your help to set boundaries and prioritize what's important to me. Give me the courage to say "NO" in a way that preserves relationships while keeping the doors open for future opportunities. Help me to let go of things I no longer have the grace to do without fear or guilt. I have lost my joy and motivation, which is leading to anxiety, depression, mood swings, and irritability.

Send Your word and heal me. I set my face like flint, and I will arise from this posture of stress and fatigue. I embrace the peace of Christ, the inner calm that comes from walking with You daily. I am refreshed in Your presence, feeling rejuvenated and invigorated as I continually endeavor to be faithful. Help me navigate change well with grace and wisdom. I recognize *and* treasure what is excellent [identifying the best and distinguishing moral differences]. Thank you for lifting the standard.

I am committed to reframing my perspective, focusing on the lessons learned, and acknowledging my potential for recovery. I do not let feelings of guilt or worthlessness define my journey; instead, I cultivate a mindset of growth and resilience. I eagerly anticipate the peace and restoration that lie ahead. In Christ, I find rest, renewal, and blessed quiet for my soul. I choose to cultivate joy in the Lord as a foundational aspect of my outlook. I build my resilience and maintain a constructive approach, even in challenging situations. You are my anchor in every storm. You restore, confirm, strengthen, and establish me once again.

Scriptures: Is. 40:29; Col. 3:15; Phil.1:9-11; Is. 50:7; Is. 59:19; Heb. 6:19

Miracle Manifestations

Miracle Manifestations

I thank You for the miracle manifestation in my life. It leaves no trace or evidence of sickness and disease. You promised I would do greater work and more work than You. As I imitate You, Father, do the work through me. Let signs and wonders follow me because I can do all things through Christ who strengthens me. When I lay hands on the sick in Jesus' name, manifest Your healing power. When I raise the dead in Your name, manifest Your healing power.

When I cast out devils in Jesus' name, manifest Your healing power. When I pray in Jesus' name, manifest Your healing power so You may be glorified on the earth. Jesus, Your name is above all sickness, disease, and evil powers. Every knee must bow at the name of Jesus. Let the miracles manifest in every area of my life and in everything I do. I am a willing vessel at Your disposal. Lord, use me. Thank you for the anointing upon my life for signs, wonders, and miracles. Manifest Your *kairos* moments for Your people beyond and outside the confines of chronos time. Affirm their deep personal trust and confidence in Your power, and it will be exactly as they desire.

Scriptures: Matt. 15:21-28

Pick Up Your Mat and Walk

I am determined to pick up my mat and walk. I refuse to remain stagnant in the same position I've been in for years. No longer will I wallow in self-pity or make excuses for my inability to move. I take responsibility for my own life and stop blaming others for my problems. God is my shield, my Glory, and the one who lifts my head high. Lift me out of the slimy pit, out of the mud and mire, and set my feet on the rock. Please give me a firm foundation to stand on. I am ready for my miracle.

Scriptures: Ps. 40:12; Ps. 3:3, Gen 13:14; Ps 24:7; 1 Tim 2:8

Security and Protection

The Full Armor of God

I am strong in the Lord and in the power of His might. I put on the whole armor of God so that I may be able to stand against the wiles of the devil. For I do not wrestle against flesh and blood, but against principalities, against powers, against the rulers of the darkness of this age, against spiritual hosts of wickedness in the heavenly places. Therefore, I take up the whole armor of God, that I may be able to withstand in the evil day, and having done all, to stand. I stand therefore, having girded my waist with truth, having put on the breastplate of righteousness, and having shod my feet with the preparation of the gospel of peace; above all, taking the shield of faith with which I will be able to quench all the fiery darts of the wicked one. And take the helmet of salvation and the sword of the Spirit, which is the Word of God.

Scriptures: Eph. 6:10-17

An Ever-Present Help

God is my refuge and strength, an ever-present help in trouble. LORD, do not be far from me. Come quickly to help me. You are a fortress of salvation for Your anointed ones. The LORD is my strength and shield; my heart trusts in You, and You help me. My heart overflows and leaps for joy, and I lift my voice in song; I praise You. You, Lord God, are my Strength, my personal bravery, and my invincible army. You make my feet like hinds' feet and make me walk and not stand still in terror but walk and make spiritual progress upon my high places of trouble, suffering, and responsibility!

Scriptures: Ps. 46:1; Ps. 22:19; Ps. 28:7-8; Hab. 3:17-19

Accidents

Father, we decree and declare that _____ will live and not die, but declare the Word of the Lord. We decree the Zoe life of Christ flows through _____ body. We command angels to invade the room of _____ in the name of Jesus. Father, You sent Your word and healed _____. Just like You called Lazarus forth from the grave, we call _____ back from the dead. Father, You said eyes have not seen, and ears have not heard, nor has it entered into the heart of man the things which God has prepared for those who love Him. Comfort and guide us in this circumstance, Lord, because every single one of Your promises is yes and amen. We thank you for the resurrection power of Your Word and the evidence of it in _____ life.

Scriptures: Ps. 118:17; Ps. 107:20; John 11:43; 2 Cor. 1:20

Help Me Lord

God, You came so I could have life and life more abundantly. Your words are life and health to my flesh, and they prosper my health, life, and soul. Please help me to find rest for my weary soul. Forgive me of my sin. Please heal me. Strengthen me. Help me. And uphold me with Your righteous right hand.

Scriptures: John 10:10; Prov. 4:22; 1 John 1:9; Is. 41:10

Enemies

Lord, help me not fret because of evildoers, nor be envious of the wicked, evil men, as You will put out the lamp of the wicked one. Comfort my heart, though, Lord, as they do evil against me, even those I call my friends. Anoint my head in the presence of my enemies and prepare a table before me. While I don't feel like it, I give my enemy bread to eat, and if he/she is thirsty, I give him water to drink. I pray for my enemies and love them. God, You are greater than any enemy that I have. When my ways, please You, make my enemies to be at peace with me. God, help me as I desire to bear fruit in this situation and bring glory to Your name.

Scriptures: Prov. 15:7; John 15:8; Matt. 5:44; Prov. 24:19-20; Ps. 23:5; Prov. 25:21-22

The Angel of the Lord

The angel of the Lord is very near and encamps around me because I respect and obey the Lord. He keeps me safe from danger and delivers me. You are my hiding place and refuge, preserving me from trouble and distress. You surround me with triumphant shouts of deliverance. Whatever I do and wherever I go, You, Lord, ensure my safety in all my endeavors. You preserve my going out and my coming in from this time forth, eternity, and even forevermore. With the Lord by my side, I am always secure because the Lord will always keep me safe.

Scriptures: Ps 34:7; Ps. 32:7; Ps. 128:1

Touch Not My Anointed

God has a remarkable purpose and an extraordinary plan for my life that even the devil can't destroy without my express consent and permission. I am chosen for a specific purpose, a unique mission on earth with an anointing from the Holy One. I am set apart, specially gifted, prepared, and empowered by the Holy Spirit.

God firmly established and confirmed me in joint fellowship with Christ. He has anointed, equipped, and empowered me with the gifts of the Spirit. I am sealed, certified, and dedicated for a specific vital purpose by the Holy Spirit in my heart, as a divine pledge, much like a security deposit to guarantee the fulfillment of His promise of eternal life. Therefore, no one and nothing can touch me. Your Word boldly declares, "Touch not my anointed ones."

As a result, my future victory is certain, sure, definite, guaranteed, unquestionable, and indisputable, allowing me to stand my ground with unwavering confidence. I remain steadfast, immovable, strong, and steady, always excelling in the Lord's work. I always do my best, go above and beyond, do more than is needed, exceed expectations, and never hold back. I continually know that my labor, even when exhausted, is not futile nor wasted and never without purpose.

Scriptures: 1 Chron. 16:21-22; 1 John 2:20; 2 Cor. 1:21-22

Protection From My Enemies

Father, I am Your Beloved. Therefore, protect me from my enemies. I have obeyed Your voice and do all that You speak as You commanded me. I will not be afraid of them because You are with me. When the enemy comes in like a flood, lift up a standard against him. You are an enemy to my enemies and an adversary to my adversaries. Oppose those who oppose me. Though I walk in the midst of trouble, You preserve my life. You stretch out Your hand against the anger of my foes.

With Your right hand, You save me. Please take pleasure in me and cause my enemies to make peace with me. I will not repay evil with evil or insult with insult. I repay evil with blessings so that I may inherit a blessing. I do not gloat when my enemy falls. I do not let my heart rejoice when they stumble. As You commanded, I feed my enemy if they are hungry. I give them something to drink because they are thirsty. Then, You validate my life in the clear light of day and stamp me with Your approval. You make my innocence radiate as the dawn and justice shine like the noonday sun.

Scriptures: Is. 59:19; Exo. 23:22; Ps. 138:7; Prov. 16:7; 1 Pet. 3:9-14; Prov. 24:17; Rom. 12:20; Ps. 37:6

Anoint My Head in My Enemy's Presence

Allow my enemies to live long enough to witness the blessings You bestow upon me. Increase Your anointing in my life. Let the oil flow abundantly down my head, face, hands, heart, and feet. Let there be a continuous supply of Your oil so it is evident that it is not by my might, nor by my power, but by Your Spirit, God's Spirit, of which the oil is a symbol. You are the source of my strength.

You have chosen the foolish things of this world to put to shame the wise, the weak things to shame the mighty, and the lowly and overlooked things of this world, and the things which are despised, and the things which are not, to bring to nothing the things that are. Let no flesh glory in Your presence. You are the hope of glory within me. Even though I am not as experienced and qualified as others, let confidence and boldness flow out of me because I have been in Your presence. Thank you for the sweatless victories that confirm Your presence in my life and that You are with me.

Scriptures: 1 Cor. 1:26-29; Zec. 4:6; Acts 4:13

Divine Protection While Traveling

I confidently dwell in the secret place of the Most-High and abide under the shadow of the Almighty. For You alone, O Lord, make me dwell in safety. Your name is a strong tower. I run to it, and You keep me safe from all harm. You watch over my coming and going now, always, and forevermore. Your faithful promises are my shield, armor, and protection. You command Your angels concerning me to guard me carefully.

I can lie down in peace and sleep confidently. You preserve the way of Your saints and the peace of God, which surpasses all understanding, guards my heart and mind through Christ Jesus. You have not given me a spirit of fear, but of power, love, and a sound mind. Therefore, not a single hair on my head shall be lost or harmed when I travel by airplane, bicycle, boat, bus, car, ferry, helicopter, limousine, motorcycle, train, truck, van, or any other mode of transportation. You have given me the authority to trample on serpents and scorpions and over all the power of the enemy, and nothing shall by any means hurt me.

You lead me on the right path and establish my steps. Lord, deliver me from every evil work and preserve me for Your heavenly kingdom. You leave me with peace and grant me Your perfect peace. Therefore, I refuse to let my heart be troubled or afraid. Instead, I travel with courage and strength, embracing Your perfect peace, which empowers and equips me to navigate and overcome every challenging situation and circumstance I face.

Scriptures: Ps. 91; Ps. 4:8; Prov. 2:8; 2 Tim. 4:18; Phil 4:7; 2 Tim. 1:7; Luke 10:19; Luke 21:18; Prov. 3:21-25; Luke 4:10; Prov. 3:23-24; Ps. 121:7-8; Ps. 23; Prov. 16:9; John 14:27

God's Divine Protection

I am precious in Your sight. You honor and love me beyond measure. You promise me victory, which fills my heart with boldness and courage. Therefore, I refuse to fear because You have redeemed me. You have called me by my name. I am proudly Yours. I belong to You. When the enemy comes in like a flood, the Spirit of the Lord will lift up a standard against him. When I pass through the waters, You will be with me, and through the rivers, they shall not overflow me. When I walk through the fire, I shall not be burned, nor shall the flame scorch me, for You are the Lord my God, The Holy One of Israel, my Savior. I confidently and boldly walk forward, empowered by knowing who I am and whose I am.

Scriptures: Is. 43:1-5; Is. 59:19

The Lord Is My Shepherd

The Lord is my Shepherd; I shall not want. You make me lie down in green pastures; You lead me beside the still waters. You restore my soul; You lead me in the paths of righteousness for Your name's sake. Yea, though I walk through the valley of the shadow of death, I will fear no evil, for You are with me; Your rod and Your staff, they comfort me. You prepare a table before me in the presence of my enemies; You anoint my head with oil; My cup runs over. Surely goodness and mercy shall follow me all the days of my life. And I will dwell in the house of the Lord, forever.

Scriptures: Ps. 23

The Choice Weapon of My Warfare

Father, You are my choice weapon of warfare. When I pray or call on You, You promise to answer me. My enemies trouble me greatly and relentlessly seek my defeat and downfall. I continually seek Your divine presence and guidance, confidently knowing that You will provide me with the strategy to win the battle against my enemies. You are the Lord of the Breakthrough. Empower me to sweep away my enemies like a flood of water. Accomplish this mission through me, and I will continually ask You for a new strategy against my enemies that ensures my perpetual victories.

You have always prospered me for a specific reason and unique purpose throughout my entire life. I am deeply grateful for the honor and success You have bestowed upon me. I will use this platform to bring You all the glory, all the honor, and all the praise. Oh, that You would bless me abundantly indeed, and enlarge my territory, that Your hand would be with me, and that You would keep me from all evil and harm, that I may not cause pain and anguish! I humbly ask You to grant me this request and let my gift bring me before great men who will use their power, ability, influence, and nobility on my behalf. May my fame spread throughout all the earth and bring fear upon those who dare to touch Your anointed. Surely, it will come to pass.

Scriptures: 1 Chron. 14:1-17; 1 Chron. 4:10; Jer. 33:3; Ps. 6:6-7

Restoration And Renewal

Refreshing Others

Please help me to have a spirit that refreshes others anytime and anywhere distressing spirits appear. I am the thermostat that shifts the atmosphere. I confidently perform spiritual CPR that causes spiritual revival. Help me to soothe the savage beast. May a spiritual revival occur in their heart and cause their baby to leap. Help me to maintain a joyful heart and spirit that encourages others. May others find joy, peace, and rest in my presence. May my happy heart be refreshing to others.

Please help me to restore and revive all who encounter me. May my presence increase their chance of survival and prevent spiritual death. My love and loyalty are inspirational and draw all men to God. My generosity of spirit replenishes and revives the spirit of others. My uplifting attitude and temperance are an energizing influence. I am an ambassador of joy, encouragement, love, and a helpful attitude, which leaves a lasting uplifting deposit. Hope is renewed and revived as You use me to touch the lives of others.

Scriptures: Prov. 11:24; Luke 1:41-42; Prov. 17:22

Transformation

Create in me a pure heart, O God, and renew a steadfast spirit within me. Do not cast me away from Your presence or take Your Holy Spirit from me. Restore to me the joy of Your salvation, grant me a willing spirit, and sustain me.

Scriptures: Ps. 51: 10-12

Suddenly

In the midst of my trials and tribulations, I fervently pray, praise, and sing hymns to God, knowing that He is listening to my every word. I refuse to succumb to fear or be immobilized and paralyzed by my circumstances. I will not be seized with alarm. As I lifted up my voice and wept, suddenly, You heard my cry and saw my tears, answering me unexpectedly and swiftly. You are the one who sees me. The fulfillment of Your promise gives me the strength to rise above my challenges. I will arise, get up, and soar above my experiences! I will arise from the depression and prostration in which circumstances have kept me—rise to a new life! I will shine and be radiant with the glory of the Lord, for my light has come, and the glory of the Lord has risen upon me!

Scriptures: Gen. 21:16-18; Acts 16:25-34; Is. 60:1

Broken Chains

Repentance brought me a divine appointment with my destiny. Chains that once bound me have been broken in my life. Like clay in the potter's hand, my mindset shifted and completely transformed. I've broken new ground, forged a new path, and removed obstacles that previously held me back. Now, better decisions determine my outcomes, allowing me to love in a more excellent way. A better day awaits me because royal blood flows through my veins. I am grateful for Your relentless love that results in my renewal, restoration, and recovery. With this hope for the future, I worship You forever, my God.

Scriptures: Jer. 18:6; John 3:16-17; Ps. 103:11; Rom. 8:38-39; Rom. 12:1-2

Remove the Veil/Sealed to the Day of Redemption

Everyone who practices sin is a slave to sin. Father, You care for those who have lost their life and fortune to impulsive, loose, and immoral living such as stealing, drug dealing, prostitution, pimping, breaking and entering, assault, drunk and impaired driving, fornication, illicit sex, homosexuality, idolatry, sorcery, hostility, quarreling, jealously, angry outbursts, selfish ambition, dissension, division, envy, drunkenness, wild parties, wickedness, and all manner of evil, etc.

Father, You desire that they will inherit the Kingdom of God. Remove the veil from their eyes and help them come to their senses so they can fulfill the destiny, plan, and purpose You have for their lives and not die. Your son, Jesus, paid the debt, making salvation a free gift. Position me in the right places so I can win a significant number of souls for Your glory. Help me to remain bold and courageous when I am rejected for sharing You. When they confess their sins, You are faithful and just to forgive them of their sins and cleanse them from all unrighteousness.

We will rejoice and celebrate each individual, just as You rejoice in heaven over one sinner who repents. Seal them to the day of redemption as they embrace repentance, the turnaround, and transformation in their lives. I will go as You commanded me and make disciples of all nations, baptizing them in the name of the Father and of the Son and of the Holy Spirit, teaching them to observe all that You have commanded me, so they are continually transformed into Your image.

Scriptures: Eph. 4:30; Luke 15:7; 2 Cor. 3:14; Acts 11:24; Gal. 5:19-21; Rom. 8:29; 2 Cor. 3:18; John 8:31-38

The Fountain of Living Waters

Father, Your Spirit gives life. I summon the living waters to refresh, rejuvenate, and invigorate me. I desire to drink deeply from this living water so I will never be thirsty again. Let it continually become a fresh, bubbling spring within me, giving me eternal life. Satisfy my thirst for You. Equip and empower me to remain energized and active in my growth so I can continually flow in You.

You are the source of every good and perfect gift. Grant me spiritual blessings and gifts. I am a generous person and a source of blessing, so I am prosperous and enriched. Because I water others, I will be watered as well, reaping the generosity I have sown, and rivers of living water will flow out of my belly.

Lord, guide me continually. Give me water when I am thirsty and parched, and restore my strength. Then I will be like a well-watered garden, like an ever-flowing spring. I will be like a tree planted by the streams of water that yields its fruit in its season, and its leaf does not wither. All that I do prospers. The water that feeds and nourishes me flows from Your holy temple, and the fruit from these trees provides food. The leaves make sick people well and heal them.

You are the Alpha and the Omega, the beginning and the end. To all who are thirsty, You freely give the water of life. I ask You to pour out Your spirit upon my children and Your blessing upon my offspring. We eagerly receive the water of life freely so we will never have to thirst again.

Scriptures: John 4:14; Prov. 11:25; John 7:38; Ezk. 47:12; Ps. 1:3; Rev. 21:6; Is. 44:3; Is. 58:11; James 1:7

New Heaven and New Earth

I pay close attention now. You are creating new heavens and a new earth. All the earlier troubles, chaos, and pain are things of the past to be forgotten. I look ahead with joy. I anticipate what You are creating. You will make Jerusalem a source of sheer joy, and You will make Your people a pure delight. You take joy in Jerusalem and take delight in Your people.

No more sounds of weeping in the city, no cries of anguish. No more babies dying in the cradle or old people who do not enjoy a full lifetime. One hundredth birthdays will be considered normal—anything less will seem like a cheat. Then, I will build houses and move in. Then, I will plant fields and eat what I grow. No more building a house that some outsider takes over. No more planting fields that some enemy can confiscate.

For Your people will be as long-lived as trees. As Your chosen ones, I will have satisfaction in my work. I won't work and have nothing come of it; I won't have my children snatched out from under me, for I am a planting blessed by God, with my children and grandchildren likewise, God-blessed. Before I call out,

You will answer. Before I finish speaking, You will have heard me.

Scriptures: Is. 65:17-25

Victory Through Christ

This is the day of the LORD's victory; I will be happy. I will rejoice and celebrate! Give me success, O LORD! Bless me, Lord, because I come in Your name! With God, I gain the victory. I win because He defeats my enemies. The victory truly belongs to the Lord. Thanks be to God, who gives me victory and always causes me to triumph through my Lord Jesus Christ. I am more than a conqueror through Christ, who loves me immensely.

Scripture: Ps. 108:13; Rom. 8:37; Prov. 21;31; 1 Cor. 15:57; Prov. 21;31; Ps. 118:24-29

Triumph Over Mental Challenges

Stress and Anxiety

I take authority over stress, anxiety, panic attacks, and feelings of spinning out of control. I have the mind of Christ. You are my Counselor, Helper, Intercessor, Advocate, Strengthener, and Standby. You are the *Parakletos*; the one called to come alongside me. Make haste to help me, Lord. Thank you for keeping me in perfect peace. I will not let my heart be troubled, and I will not be afraid.

Scriptures: 1 Cor. 2:16; John 14:26; Ps. 70:1; Is. 26:3; John 14:27

When Feeling Overwhelmed

God, thank you for being my strength, fortress, and refuge daily, especially when I feel tired, stressed, and completely overwhelmed. You said You would instruct me and teach me the way I should go, and counsel me with Your loving eye. Father, Your heart rejoices when my heart is wise because knowledge and wisdom are sweet to my soul. Help me always to choose this path and speak the right things.

Scriptures: Ps. 18:2; Ps. 32:8; Prov. 2:10

Exhaustion and Stress

Thank you, God, for being my constant strength and refuge, especially during times of exhaustion and stress. When I feel completely overwhelmed, You are a wonderful comfort and refuge. You promise to guide me and impart wisdom. You are my source of reassurance.

Scriptures: Ps. 46:1; James 1:5

Worry and Anxiety

I won't be anxious about anything, but in every situation, I let my requests be made known to God through prayer and supplication with thanksgiving. I cast my burdens on You, Lord, and You will sustain me. You will never permit the righteous to be moved. You did not give me a spirit of fear but of power, love, and self-control. You give me peace unlike anything the world has ever seen and cannot give me.

I will not let my heart be troubled, neither will I let it be afraid. The peace of God, which surpasses all understanding, guards my heart and mind in Christ Jesus. I will not be anxious about tomorrow, for tomorrow will worry about itself. I will not be anxious about my life, what I will eat or drink, nor about my body or what I will wear. Birds neither sow nor reap nor have a storehouse or barn, yet God feeds them all. I am more valuable than birds! Now,

God, give me peace at all times, in every way, and be with me.

Scriptures: Phil. 4:6-7; 1 Pet. 5:7; Ps. 55:22; 2 Tim. 1:7; John 14:27; Matt. 6:34; Matt. 6:25-26

Pride

I repent for thinking more highly of myself than I should. All that I am and all that I have is because of You and not because of my own efforts, talents, and abilities. I am not puffed up. I am a humble person. You will not find pride, arrogance, conceit, smugness, self-importance, and egotism in me. It only leads to a damaged reputation and brings disgrace, dishonor, shame, and humiliation. I seek guidance to avoid being critical of others, demeaning, divisive, slanderous, disrespectful, resentful, contentious, argumentative, unteachable, and having a superior attitude.

I strive to embody humility and understanding. I exercise humility characterized by skillfulness, godly wisdom, and soundness of mind. Shaped by trials, I have learned to walk humbly with God, remaining teachable. I will not be proud and arrogant in my heart because it is disgusting, hateful, and exceedingly offensive to the Lord, and it will not go unpunished by him. Search me, O God, and know my heart; test me and know my anxious thoughts. Point out anything in me that offends You and leads me along the path of everlasting life. Your grace is sufficient for me, and Your power is made perfect in my weakness.

Scriptures: Rom. 12:3; 1 Tim. 6:4; 1 Cor. 4:18; Ps. 139: 23-24; 2 Cor. 12:9

Overcoming Intimidation and Fear

I will not for a moment be frightened or intimidated by my opponents and adversaries, for such constancy and fearlessness will be a clear sign, proof, and seal to them of their impending destruction but a sure token and evidence of my deliverance and salvation from God. The fear of man brings a snare. Therefore, I will lean on, trust in, and put my confidence in the Lord, who will keep me safe and set me on high.

For God, You did not give me a spirit of timidity, cowardice, or fear. You have given me a spirit of power, love, sound judgment, and personal discipline, abilities that result in a calm, well-balanced mind and self-control. I will be strong and courageous. I will not fear or dread them, for You, oh Lord, go before me and with me. You will not leave me nor forsake me. You, Lord, fight for me. Your shield of faith will extinguish all the flaming darts of the evil one. You will strengthen, help, and uphold me with Your righteous right hand. Therefore, I will be as bold as a lion.

Scriptures: Phil 1:28; Prov. 29:25; 2 Tim. 1:7; Deut. 3:22; Is. 41:10; Prov. 28:1; Eph. 6:16

Anxiety

Father, comfort me in my affliction, for I know that Your promise gives me life. Help me to overcome a crushed spirit that dries up the bones, significant mental distress, anguish, agony, grief, misery, self-harm, and suffering. Please help me conquer anxiety disorders that manifest themselves in excessive fear, worry, and panic attacks. Remove depressed moods, so I don't feel sad, irritable, or empty. Please help me find joy in activities again so that I won't focus on my problems.

Help me to triumph over agitation, persistent delusions, hallucinations, and disorganized thinking. Don't allow me to relive past trauma. Block intrusive thoughts, flashbacks, and nightmares of traumatic events that haunt me. When I am overcome with feelings of excessive guilt, low self-worth, and hopelessness, remind me about the beautiful future that You have for me. Disrupt thoughts of death and suicide.

Grant me sweet sleep so I don't feel tired or low in energy. Increase my appetite for food. Lift me up because I am bowed down. Take away this sickness from me. Strengthen me. Heal me. Prosper me in my soul. You said a healed heart is a good medicine. You, God, are the most effective prevention and treatment option available for me that does not leave uncomfortable side effects.

Regulate my thoughts, emotions, and behaviors. Wipe every tear from my eyes so that there will be no more death, mourning, crying, or pain, for the old things have passed away, and all things have been made new. Father, just as You heard David's prayer and saw his tears and healed him, do the same for me. According to Nahum 1:9, Lord, end this torment completely so this affliction will not arise a second time. Everything is already all right. Today is the last day that I have suffered from anxiety.

Scriptures: Ps. 119:50; Prov. 18:14; Jer. 29:11; Prov. 3:24; Ps. 146:8; Exo. 23:25; 3 John 1:2; Prov. 17:22; Rev. 21:4; Nah. 1:9; Ps. 6:6-7

Overcoming Stinking Thinking

I bind all negative thoughts that will cause me to doubt the good plans God has for me. You plan to prosper me and give me a future and a hope. You will not harm me. Before You formed me in my mother's womb, You knew me. Before I was born, You consecrated me and set me apart. You appointed me a prophet to the nations. Your plans for me stand firm forever; the purposes of Your heart through all generations. I was born for such a time as this, equipped to handle whatever comes my way because You said, "You will never leave me nor forsake me."

All the curses in my bloodline ended with my parents. I receive all the blessings that God has for me by faith. I cast down every thought that exalts itself against the knowledge of God. Stinking thinking, negative and irrational thoughts, be gone! I refuse to embrace thoughts that are harmful, destructive, depressing, discouraging, pessimistic, or damaging about myself. I fill my mind with thoughts about good things.

I fix my thoughts and meditate on whatever is true, whatever is honorable and worthy of respect, whatever is right and confirmed by God's word, whatever is pure and wholesome, whatever is lovely and brings peace, whatever is admirable, noble, and reputable; the best, not the worst; the beautiful, not the ugly; things to praise, not things to curse. I think continually about these things, center my mind on them, and implant them in my heart.

The thief comes only to steal, kill, and destroy. But Jesus came that I may have and enjoy life, and have it in abundance [to the full, till it overflows]. I give all my worries and cares to God, for He cares about me. I must stay alert! I watch out for my great enemy, the devil. He prowls around like a roaring lion, seeking someone to devour. I stand firm against him and be strong in my faith. I belong to God. I have already won the victory! The Spirit of God lives in me and is greater than the spirit who lives in the world.

I have the overwhelming victory through Christ, who loves me. And I am convinced that nothing can ever separate me from God's love. Not death nor life, neither angels nor demons, neither my fears for today nor my worries about tomorrow—not even the powers of hell can separate me from God's love. No power in the sky above or in the earth below—indeed, nothing in all creation will ever be able to separate me from the love of God that is revealed in Christ Jesus our Lord.

Scriptures: Jer. 29:11; Jer. 1:5; Deut. 31:8; Ps. 33:11; Esther 4:14; Gal. 3:14; 2 Cor. 10:5-7; Phil. 4:8; John 10:10; 1 Pet. 5:7-9; 1 John 4:4; Rom. 8:37; Rom. 8:31-29

Emotional Instability/Unstable Mind

I am just like You because You are the same yesterday, today, and forever. Therefore, I am not easily disturbed or upset. I am always cool, calm, and collected. I have a stable personality and am not prone to sudden and shifting mood changes. I am not emotionally unstable. I am sane and rational and do not fluctuate in my emotions. God has given me a spirit of self-control.

I am mentally and emotionally sound. I am well-balanced, sensible, and reasonable. I am unwavering in my decisions. I make good, sound, and reasonable decisions. I do not make impulsive, emotionally driven decisions. I exercise good judgment based on understanding all the facts. My word is my bond. I am firmly established. I am steady in purpose, firm, and resolute. I am consistent in my approach to everything that I do. I possess the fruit of the Spirit: love, joy, peace, patience, kindness, goodness, faithfulness, gentleness, and self-control. The peace of God, which surpasses all understanding, guards my heart and my mind in Christ Jesus.

Scriptures: Heb. 13:8; John 14:27; 2 Tim. 1:7; Prov. 3:5-6; Phil. 4:7; Gal. 5:22-23; Col. 2:7

Overcoming Childhood Trauma (Bullying)

God, You are no respecter of persons. Make my name great on earth for Your sake and draw all men unto You. From my youth, I was teased unmercifully for many reasons. But You know my beginning from my end. And though my beginning was small, my latter end would greatly increase. Remove all bitterness from my soul and heal me from the trauma. Help me to love Your people unconditionally and pray for those who despitefully use me. Minimize selfish ambition, pride, and deceit. I always walk in humility. Humility is a lifestyle. Make me an effective witness for the Kingdom as I walk in agape towards everyone I encounter.

Scriptures: Rom. 2:11; John 12:32; Is. 46:10; Job 8:7; Matt. 5:44-46; Phil. 2:3; 1 Pet. 5:2-6

Overcoming Trauma

Father, help me fulfill Your vision and plan for my life. Help me to overcome every trauma that I have encountered and endured in life that has resulted in self-esteem issues, shame, and guilt. Allow me not to have flashbacks and endure crippling emotional and physical pain that results in depression, anxiety, PTSD, bipolar disorders, cutting, and emotionally unstable responses. Heal me and make me whole. Make an utter end, Lord of these afflictions, so it won't arise a second time.

Scriptures: Nah. 1:9

Breaking the Curse

Every generational curse in my bloodline is broken. This cycle stops with the generation before me. I am free. Every action, behavior, belief, conduct, habit, addiction, dependency, superstition, or tradition within my bloodline that does not glorify God is destroyed. I refuse to be bound by idolatry, disobedience, prison sentences, sickness and disease, especially depression and anxiety, witchcraft, horoscopes, poverty, verbal and physical abuse, and any kind of generational trauma.

I cast down every negative quality, trait, and characteristic of my grandparents and parents. I will not repeat their mistakes. I possess a growth mindset that causes me to reclaim all the territory stolen from me and the previous generations. I refuse to let the iniquity of my ancestors affect my children and grandchildren for generations to come. I reject the idea of passing down negative patterns to future generations.

Bring liberation, bring freedom to my family and me. I seek freedom and transformation for my family. Set the captives free. Change my family's legacy. I am in Christ; therefore, I am a new creation; old things have passed away; behold, all things have become new. Because I am a new creation in Christ, I believe in the power of renewal and liberation for every one of us from every generational curse in my bloodline.

Scriptures: 2 Cor. 10:5; Deut. 1:8; Deut. 5:9; Luke 4:18; 2 Cor. 5:17

Conquering Anger, Bitterness, Resentment, Shame, And Guilt

Guarding My Heart

Lord, enable me to let all bitterness, wrath, anger, clamor, perpetual hate, resentment, strife, fault-finding, and slander be put away from me, along with every kind of malice, all spitefulness, verbal abuse, and hostility. Inspire and motivate me to be kind and helpful to others, tender-hearted, compassionate, understanding, and forgiving towards others readily and freely, just as God in Christ also forgave me. Empower and equip me to walk in love, light, and wisdom so I do not grieve the Holy Spirit.

Above all else, empower me to guard my heart and remain vigilant because it is the wellspring of life. Everything I do flows from my heart, and it determines and influences the course and condition of everything in my life. Fill me with Your Holy Spirit, and I will speak to others in psalms, hymns, and spiritual songs, singing and making melody in my heart to the Lord, giving thanks always for all things to God the Father in the name of my Lord Jesus Christ, submitting to one another in the fear of the Lord.

Scriptures: Eph. 4:31-32; Eph. 5:18-20; Prov. 4:23

Overcoming the Root of Bitterness and Resentment

A sharp, pungent, disagreeable, and evil personality often refuses to reconcile with others. This bitterness manifests itself in spite, hostility, resentment, and hatred. It takes root deep in the heart and spreads, causing trouble and bitter torment, contaminating and defiling everyone around it.

Empower me to transform from a bitter, angry person into a forgiving one. Help me refrain from harsh words and actions that wound others. Guide me in releasing these destructive emotions. Empower me to show kindness, mercy, and forgiveness, just as I have experienced forgiveness and grace from God through Christ. I choose not to dwell on the wrongs done to me. Soften my heart so I do not spread negativity. I do not want to miss out on God's grace or make others feel bad in my presence. I choose to walk in forgiveness and love, experiencing it in every aspect of my life.

Scriptures: Heb. 12:15; Eph. 4:31-32

Seeking Forgiveness

Father, forgive me of any sin done in thought, word, or deed. I confess You as my Lord and Savior. I release all individuals who have hurt me. Heal me of all bitterness, wrath, anger, and malice against these individuals. I will not judge or condemn them. I forgive them as You have forgiven me. I promise to be kind and tenderhearted towards them. I will make forgiveness a lifestyle and forgive them continuously. Cleanse me, Lord, and make me whole. I receive the gift of the Holy Spirit.

Scriptures: 1 John 1:9; Col 3:13; Eph. 4:32; Ps. 51:1-2

Dealing With Oppression

People have taken advantage of me by exploiting my kindness and treating me unfairly and cruelly. While I feel powerless in changing my situation and circumstances and utterly oppressed by their attempts to control my future potential and define my identity, I refuse to allow negativity to take root in my mind. When I look up to the hills, I am reminded that my help comes from the Lord. I am a child of God, and You are obligated to come quickly to my aid. Though I walk in the flesh, I do not war according to the flesh, for the weapons of my warfare are not carnal but divinely powerful for the destruction of strongholds. The enemy's warfare plans stand no chance against Your well-planned response. You are the God of justice. You are a refuge for the oppressed, a place of security, survival, and hope for me. No evil deed is hidden from Your sight. When I need encouragement to persevere, You hear my cries and prepare my heart because You work righteousness and justice for all who are oppressed. The gates of hell will not prevail against me. Thank you for the divine strategy and deliverance that frees me from oppression.

Scriptures: Ps. 121:1; Ps. 10: 17; Ps. 9:9; Ps. 103:6; Matt. 16:18

Overcoming Rejection

People rejected me, but God chose me. I am precious to Him. Though my father and mother forsake me, the LORD will receive me. For the LORD will not reject His people; He will never forsake His inheritance. But He said to me, "My grace is sufficient for you, for My power is made perfect in weakness." Therefore, I will boast all the more gladly about my weaknesses so that Christ's power may rest on me. If the world hates you, remember that it hated Me first. Whoever listens to you listens to Me; whoever rejects you rejects Me; but whoever rejects Me rejects Him who sent Me. Therefore, there is no condemnation for those in Christ Jesus.

May the God of hope fill you with all joy and peace as you trust in Me so that you may overflow with hope by the power of the Holy Spirit. You created my inmost being. You knit me together in my mother's womb. I praise You because I am fearfully and wonderfully made. Your works are wonderful, and I know that full well. I cry out to You, Lord, and You hear and deliver me from all my troubles.

Anoint my head with oil in the presence of my enemies so that my cup runs over. Allow Your goodness and mercy to follow me all the days of my life, and I will dwell in the house of the Lord forever. Oh, that You would bless me indeed, and enlarge my territory, that Your hand would be with me, and that You would keep me from evil, that I may not cause pain! Lord, grant me my request because I am brokenhearted and crushed in spirit.

Scriptures: John 15:16; Is. 43:4; 2 Cor. 12:9; John 15:28-27; Rom. 8:1; Rom. 15:13; Ps. 139: 13-14; Ps. 34:17; Ps. 23:5-6; 1 Chron. 4:10

Addressing Shame and Guilt

When I look in the mirror, I am assaulted and overwhelmed with shame, guilt, and hopelessness. I struggle with emotions that make me feel bad, dirty, vile, worthless, and insignificant, which leads to guilt, rejection, and feelings of inadequacy. I choose to exchange my shame to receive a double portion instead of grace and rejoice in Your inheritance. I renew my mind daily with the Word of God to change and reshape my faulty beliefs and thoughts about myself. I have the mind of Christ. I refuse to believe the enemy's lies about me and the strongholds that resist the truth and perpetuate deep-seated beliefs about myself.

I use God's mighty weapons, God's truth, to replace the enemy's lies, knock down the strongholds of human reasoning, and destroy false arguments. I prioritize prayer, meditation on God's Word, and speaking positive affirmations as strategies that affirm and reinforce my identity in Christ and guard my mind. I no longer engage in negative self-talk. Instead, I capture rebellious, unhealthy thoughts and teach them to obey Christ. I am destined to live and live more abundantly because anyone who believes in You will never be put to shame. I am in Christ; therefore, I am a new creation. Old things have passed away; behold, all things have become new.

Consequently, I reject condemnation because there is no longer any condemnation for those in Christ. I commit to walking in the Spirit and embracing the freedom that comes with it. I walk in peace, health, wholeness, and prosperity in my mind. I am a Spirit-empowered believer living a transformed life.

Scriptures: Is. 61:7; Rom.10:11; Rom. 8:1; Rom. 12:2; John 10:10; 2 Cor. 10:5

No More Condemnation

The devil is an accuser of the brethren. He comes to steal, kill, and destroy, but You came that I may have life and have life more abundantly. I will no longer feel guilt, shame, and condemnation over my sins and moral failures. I will no longer feel unworthy. I ask for Your forgiveness and confess my sins to You because You are faithful and just to forgive me of my sins and cleanse me from all unrighteousness.

Now, there is no condemnation because I am a new creature in Christ Jesus. I receive Your love and times of refreshing that come from the Lord. I am a new creation. Old things have passed away; behold, all things have become new. I choose to renew my mind every day to maintain my freedom. Thank you for Your daily mercies that refresh my spirit.

Scriptures: Rom. 8:1; John 10:10; 1 John 1:9; Acts 3:19-23

Triumph Over Grief, Loss, And Mourning

Overcoming Grief And Loss

You, Lord, stand close to the brokenhearted and save those crushed in spirit. Your peace You leave with me, and Your peace You give to me. Not as the world gives, do You give to me. I refuse to let my heart be troubled or afraid. Though my flesh and heart may fail, God is my heart's strength and portion forever. Weeping may last through the night, but joy comes in the morning. I am blessed when I mourn because I will be comforted.

Grief is a journey, and I won't stay down. I choose to take action. I choose to trust God even when I don't understand and the path is unclear. I will reach out and help others who face this same challenge. I will call or video chat with someone or write a letter to someone in prison. I will sow seeds of kindness or money to those in need, as well as support ministries. I will watch uplifting movies, enjoy a comedy show, and engage in other uplifting activities that bring me joy and laughter. Then, You will transform my mourning into joyful dancing. You have taken away my mourning clothes and clothed me with joy so I might sing praises to You and not be silent. O Lord my God, I will give You thanks forever.

You are the Resurrection and the Life. Anyone who believes in You will live, even though they die. I look forward to one day when You will wipe away every tear from my eyes, and death shall be no more, neither shall there be mourning, nor crying, nor pain anymore, for all the former things have passed away. I hear You saying, "Now, get up! Arise! It is Your duty, and I am with You. Be strong, be brave, and take action!"

Scripture: John 11:25; Rev. 21:4; Matt. 5:4; John 14:27; Ps. 73:26; Ps. 34:18; Ps. 30:11; Ezra 10:4

Overcoming Grief and Mourning

Father, console me as I mourn; give me beauty for ashes, the oil of joy for mourning, and the garment of praise for the spirit of heaviness. Heal my broken heart. You promise to wipe away every tear from my eyes. I will not be discouraged. I will not allow my heart to be sad. I will put my hope in God! I will praise You again —my Savior and my God! I believe Your promise that You are the Resurrection and the Life. Those who believe in You, even though they die, will live, and everyone who lives and believes in You will never die.

Therefore, I will not let my heart be troubled. You promised You would never leave me nor forsake me. You are close to the brokenhearted, and save those crushed in spirit. When my flesh and my heart fail, God is the strength of my heart and my portion forever. I am blessed and empowered to prosper when I mourn because You comfort me. I receive Your peace and will not let my heart be troubled. I will not be afraid because You comfort and defend me. Blessed be the Lord who has not left me without a redeemer.

Scriptures: Is. 61:3; Rev. 21:4; Ps. 119:114; John 11:25-26; John 14:4; Heb. 13:5; Ps. 34:18; Ps. 73:26; Matt. 5:4; Ruth 4:14

Overcoming Painful Thoughts of Despair and Discouragement

Lord, You came that I might live, and have life more abundantly. My life and world feel dark, empty, and hopeless. The pain is so unbearable. I am in desperate need of Your guidance to pivot and navigate from relentless thoughts of death and dangerous behaviors. Equip and empower me to have unshakeable confidence in You. You are the God of hope; fill me with all joy and peace so I can abound in hope by the power of the Holy Spirit. No situation is beyond Your redemptive power and transformative grace. You have a complete blueprint for my life and a strategy to help me overcome my struggles through courage and faith. I need to hear Your voice clearly, so I do not make the wrong decisions, but instead make wise choices that allow me to experience the life You envisioned and planned for me. For Your thoughts toward me are thoughts of peace and not of evil, to give me a future and a hope. Please align my path with Your purpose and perfect will for my life.

Scriptures: Rom. 15:13; Jer. 29:11; Prov. 13:12.

Dominion Over Depression

Life has its challenges, full of ups and downs, and I've certainly faced my share of difficulties recently. Yet, in the midst of my overwhelming and persistent sadness, anxiety, despair, emptiness, hopelessness, and pessimism about my life, You are my guiding light, restoring my soul. Lately, the people around me — my family, friends, and coworkers — often contribute to my restlessness and frustration, making me crave solitude.

I really want to be left alone, but Your Spirit is everywhere I go. I cannot escape Your presence. If I go up to heaven, You will be there. If I go down to the place of death, You will be there. If I go east, where the sun rises, or go to live in the west beyond the sea, even there, You will take my hand and lead me forward. I cannot hide from You, no matter how hard I try.

Lately, I have had more losses than victories. All hell seems to be breaking loose in my life, overwhelming me with feelings of guilt, worthlessness, and helplessness. I feel like I have disappointed my family, friends, coworkers, and even You. At times, I want to sleep and not wake up because my spirit is so crushed under the weight of it all. I have trouble falling asleep, sometimes struggle to stay asleep, and at other times, I wake up too early. You promised to give Your beloved sweet sleep.

You, LORD, are a shield around me, my glory, the One who lifts my head high. Help me not to be overwhelmed by the darkness in my life. Let Your light shine forth in my life. Help me embrace Your vision for my life, a life of abundance, with plans to prosper me and give me a future and hope. I will think about those things that are excellent and worthy of praise. I even envision lying down in green pastures and beside still waters.

I solemnly commit to finding joy in You, Lord, even during the trials that overwhelm me. I will fill my heart with Your Holy Spirit, allowing it to overflow with songs of praise. I will speak Your words of Scripture, sing Psalms of praise, and let the Spirit inspire spontaneous songs. This intentional posture of joy will fortify my spirit, fostering resilience and optimism even in the face of adversity. I take dominion over depression.

Lord, allow Your hand to come upon me, grant me Your supernatural strength, and gird up my loins for the challenges ahead. Hear my cry and lift me out of this slimy depressive pit of despair, out of the mud and mire. Set my feet on the solid rock and give me a firm foundation to stand on. Put a new song in my mouth, a song of hope and renewal. Oh! May the God of hope fill me up with all joy, shower me with all peace, and fill me with the life-giving energy of the Holy Spirit, overflowing with hope!

Scriptures: Ps. 139:7-12; Ps. 23:3; Jer. 29:11; Phil. 4:8; Ps. 40:3; Phil. 4:8; Ps. 3:3; Ps. 34:18; Rom. 15:13; Eph. 5:18-19

Overwhelming Peace

Peace

Father, thank you for the peace You left for me as an inheritance and for giving it to me. Help me experience this peace regardless of the storms I encounter in life. The peace You gave me is not like the peace the world gives. I will not let my heart be troubled, and I will not be afraid. You are the vine that I cling to. I will not give up and quit. Nor will I throw in the towel. In You, I have perfect peace and confidence. I will face tribulations, trials, distress, and frustrations.

I will be of good cheer, take courage, be confident, and remain undaunted because You overcame the world and deprived it of its power to harm me and have conquered it for me. Sustain me, Lord. I surrender completely to You. Father, I am grateful for the peace that You have given me. Help me to hold on to this peace, even when I face challenges. The peace You have given me is different from the peace that the world offers. I refuse to let my heart be troubled, and I will not be afraid. I will remain connected to You like a vine. I will not give up or lose hope. In You, I find perfect peace and confidence. I know that I will encounter difficulties and frustrations, but I will remain cheerful, courageous, and confident because You have overcome the world and its power to harm me.

Lord, please sustain me. I surrender myself entirely to You so that I can experience a peace that surpasses all understanding. I will remain rooted and built up in You, firmly established in my faith, and overflowing with gratitude. You will keep me in perfect and constant peace because my mind is steadfast and focused on You. I trust in You with hope and confident expectation so I can experience the peace that passes all understanding. I remain rooted and built up in You and established in the faith, as I have been taught, abounding in it with thanksgiving. You will keep me in perfect and constant peace because my mind is steadfast, committed, and focused on You. I trust and take refuge in You with hope and confident expectation.

Scriptures: John 14:27; John 16:33; Col 2:7; Is. 26:3

Peace Is A Firm Foundation

Jesus Christ, the unchanging and eternal one, is the same yesterday, today, and forever. Therefore, I have perfect peace, and my mind is steadfast because I trust in God. The Lord is unwavering in His faithfulness. He strengthens and protects me from all evil. I am like a wise person who built his house on the rock. The rain came down, the streams rose, and the winds blew and beat against that house, yet it did not fall because it had its foundation on the rock. The Lord is my rock, my fortress, and my deliverer, in whom I take refuge. He is my shield, my stronghold, and the horn of my salvation.

I cast all my cares on the Lord, who will sustain me and never let the righteous be shaken. Therefore, I stand firm, unmoved by my circumstances. I will let nothing move me, having strapped on my feet the gospel of peace in preparation to face the enemy with firm-footed stability and the readiness produced by the good news.

I always fully dedicate myself to the work of the Lord because I confidently know that my labor is not in vain. Peace is my firm foundation, and I have no fear of bad news. My heart is steadfast, unwavering, and trusting in the Lord.

Scriptures: Heb. 13:8; Is. 26:32; 1 Thes. 3:3; Matt. 7:24-25; Ps. 18:2; Ps. 55:22; 2 Cor. 15:58; Ps. 112:7; Eph. 6:15

Victory Over the Storm

Father, I am truly thankful for Your promise that we will journey together to the other side. This assurance fills me with unwavering hope that cannot be diminished. When my heart grows faint, I call on You, confident that You will lead me to the rock that is higher than I. I will not fear bad news; my heart is steadfast, fully trusting in You. You are a stronghold for the poor and a refuge for the needy in times of distress, providing unwavering shelter from storms and shade from the heat. I cast all my anxieties upon You because You care deeply for me.

I remain alert and resolute, standing firm against the enemy who seeks to devour me. You are greater than any storm, and I know You can bring peace even in the harshest circumstances. You are my shelter and shade in times of trouble. I declare Your mercy, O God; I confidently seek Your protection and guidance, for I find refuge in You.

Scriptures: Prov. 23:18; Ps. 61:2; Ps.112:7; 2 Tim. 1:9; Heb. 6:19; 1 Pet. 4:12-13; Isaiah 4:6; John 16:33; Ps. 89:9; Ps. 107:29; Is. 25:5; Ps. 57:1; John 15:33; Ps. 112:7; Ps. 61:2; Prov. 23:18

Watch Your Mouth

Anger

I am a wise person who keeps myself under control. Only a fool fully vents their rage. I am wise and bring calm to any situation. I am swift to hear, slow to speak, slow to wrath, for the anger of man does not produce the righteousness of God that He desires. I am quick to listen, slow to speak, and slow to become angry. I am not quickly provoked in my spirit, for anger resides in the lap of fools. I will give a gentle answer to turn away wrath because a harsh word stirs up anger.

I will not act like a hot-tempered person who stirs up conflict, but I am the one who is patient and calms a quarrel. I rid myself of anger, rage, malice, slander, and filthy language from my lips. I do not make friends with people who are hot-tempered. I do not associate with anyone who is easily angered. I refrain from anger and turn from wrath. I do not fret because it only leads to evil. The evil will be destroyed, but those who hope in the LORD will inherit the land. I have great patience and understanding. I am not one who is quick-tempered and displays stupidity, foolishness, craziness, and recklessness.

Scriptures: Prov. 29:11; James 1:19-20; Ecc. 7:9; Prov. 15:1; Prov. 15:18; Prov. 22:24; Ps. 37:8-9

Set A Guard Over My Mouth

Father, set a guard, a watch over my mouth. Reckless words pierce like swords, and a wise tongue brings healing. Help me to be careful and mindful in what I do and say so I will not sin when I speak. When wicked, ungodly people are listening, I will not even open my mouth because opening my mouth will ruin everything. Keeping my mouth closed and shut will help me avoid problems and difficulties. I am not a fool who brings strife with my lips nor a tongue filled with gossip that brings tasty truffles.

Thinking before I speak protects my life and helps me avoid and stay out of trouble. When I control my tongue, I will have a long life. My lips overflow with praise, for You teach me Your decrees. I love life and desire to see good days; therefore, I will keep my tongue from evil and my lips from deceitful speech. My conversation will always be seasoned and filled with grace and salt so that I may know how to answer everyone.

Scriptures: Ps.141:3; Prov.12:18; Ps. 39:1; Prov. 13:3; Ps. 119:171; 1 Pet. 3:10; Col. 4:6

Unwholesome Talk

Unwholesome talk will not be a part of my life or come out of my mouth. I understand that what comes from my mouth defiles me, not what goes in. Therefore, I endeavor to speak with wisdom and offer faithful instruction. I will use my speech to build others up according to their needs so that it may benefit those who listen. My soothing tongue is a tree of life. I will not possess a perverse and hurtful tongue that crushes the spirit. Because my heart is righteous, I carefully consider and weigh my responses, speaking with wisdom, thoughtfulness, knowledge, and deep insight.

When I exercise restraint with my words, I am understanding and even-tempered. My tongue is not wicked nor does it secrete evil. I choose to cover an offense out of love and respect rather than repeat it and ruin a relationship. Slander has no place in me. I will remain peaceful, considerate, and gentle toward everyone. The fruit of my lips is filled with good things, and the work of my hands brings others a reward. The tongue has the power of life and death, and I eat the positive fruit of love.

Scriptures: Eph. 4:29; Matt. 15:11; Prov. 15:4; Prov. 15:28; Prov. 17:27-28; Prov. 17:19; Ps. 101:5; Titus 3:2; Prov. 12:14; Prov. 18:20-21

Financial Victory

Financial Increase

By faith, I receive the blessing of Abraham in my life. I am a descendant of Abraham. You said You will make my name great and make me a great nation. I receive these promises by faith. Because I am a tither, You rebuke the devour for my sake. You open up the windows of heaven and pour out a blessing. Your blessing is the empowerment to prosper, and the blessing of the Lord brings wealth without struggle and toil. Father, You only do wonderful things. I thank You for the financial increase in my life that brings joy, happiness, and fulfillment.

Scriptures: Gal. 3:13-14; Gen. 12:1-3; Heb. 11:8-22; Mal. 3:10-11; Prov. 10:22

Wise Steward

I am diligent in my thoughts and not hasty; therefore, plenty is attracted to me and not poverty. I use godly knowledge to fill my home with precious and pleasant riches. The Holy Spirit guides my actions and conduct. I count the cost before I begin a project or any endeavor. I tithe on all monies received. Because I am faithful in little, You can trust me with more. My hand is diligent;

therefore, I am fat and rich. I am a generous soul who lends to others as directed by the Holy Spirit. God, I ask You to multiply everything in my hand and prosper my household.

Scriptures: Prov. 21:5; Prov. 24:4; Luke 14:28-33; John 16:13; Mal. 3:8-12; Luke 16:10; Prov. 10:4

Provision

I have been young, and now I am old, yet I have not seen the righteous forsaken or his descendants begging for bread. I will not worry about what I will eat or what I will drink or what I will wear for clothing because my heavenly Father knows I need all these things. You give good gifts to Your children when we ask You! You have numbered the very hairs on my head. Therefore, I will not fear because I am more valuable than many sparrows.

Even though I have exhausted all avenues to fend for myself, I will try again as You instructed me to cast my net again on the other side. And this time, I will receive a huge harvest that I cannot contain. All grace abounds to me. I have sufficiency in everything and all things. I have an abundance of good deeds. My God shall supply all my needs according to His riches in glory in Christ Jesus.

Scriptures: Ps. 37:25; Matt. 6:25; Matt. 7:11; Luke 12:7; Matt. 10:31; John 21:6; 2 Cor. 9:18; Phil. 4:19

Sowing

When I sow, I will reap a hundredfold in the same year and be blessed by the Lord. People will see that the Lord is with me and witness the presence of the Lord upon my life and how He abundantly prospers all that is in my hand. I remember the Lord continually because He gives me the ability to create and produce wealth. When I give generously, the Lord blesses all my work, endeavors, and undertakings.

Scriptures: Deut. 8:17-18; Gen. 26:12; Prov. 3:6; Ps. 16:11; Ps. 1; Deut. 30:9

Possessing My Promise Land

Oh, bless me indeed, expand and enlarge my territory. Let Your hand be with me and shield me from evil so I may not cause pain! God, because You are the God who sees and the God who hears, grants, and fulfills my request, reward my great unwavering faith. Father, as Joshua claimed and possessed the land, I, too, shall claim and possess the land. I will enter my destined promised land.

You said I would build houses, move in, and keep living in them. I will plant fields and eat what I grow, the fruits of my labor. No outsider will take over or seize my home, land, possessions, or property. When I plant fields and vineyards, NO enemy will confiscate them. Because I am Your child, Your people, I will live and thrive as long as trees, and as Your chosen ones, I will have satisfaction and fulfillment in my work and all my endeavors, and enjoy my hard-won gains and rewards. I won't work and have nothing come of it. I will not toil in vain. My children won't be taken away from me, for I am planted, firmly rooted, and blessed by God, along with my children, my grandchildren, and all my descendants, who God has likewise blessed.

Scriptures: 1 Chron. 4:10; Heb. 10:35-36; Josh. 1:3; Jer. 29:5-11; Amos 9:15

Prosperity

Oh, Lord, grant me wisdom and understanding and give me authority wherever I go, and help my feet travel as I keep Your laws. Prosper me as I fulfill the decrees and rulings in Your Word. I will be strong and of good courage. I will not fear nor be dismayed. I am committed to righteousness and faithfulness, doing what is good and right before You, my God. In everything I do in service to You and the church, I remain obedient to Your law and commands. I will continually seek You while serving wholeheartedly, and You will prosper me abundantly.

I am like a tree planted by the waters, whose roots spread out by the river. I will not fear, falter, or cower when the heat comes. My leaves will remain green and lush, and I will not be anxious in a year of drought nor cease to yield and bear fruit. I am a blessed individual who does not walk in the counsel of the wicked. I do not stand in the way of sinners or sit in the seats of mockers.

My delight and joy are in the Law of the LORD. On Your law, I meditate day and night. I am like a tree planted by streams of water that yields its fruit in season and whose leaves do not wither. Whatever I do prospers. The Lord be magnified and exalted, who delights in the prosperity of His servant and makes His name great.

Scriptures: James 1:5; Deut. 11:24; 1 Chron. 22:13; Josh. 1:9; Prov. 21:21; 1 Kings 2:3; 2 Chron. 3:21; 2 Chron. 26:5; Gen. 12:8; Ps. 1; Ps. 35:27; Jer. 17:7-8

Tithing

I bring all my tithe to the church, that there may be food in God's house. I test You according to Your word, which says You will open for me the windows of heaven and pour out a blessing for me that there will not be room enough to receive it. After I tithe, I put aside money for myself and save so I may prosper and collection agencies will not seek me.

Scriptures: Mal. 3:8-12

Stewardship

I am committed to being a good and faithful steward who takes care of the resources and assets entrusted to me. I invest wisely in whatever is placed in my care. Your Word says when I am faithful with a few things, You will entrust me with greater responsibilities. I will not be a wicked, lazy, negligent, or unproductive steward. I desire to increase and grow. Therefore, I invest the resources You have given me so I can receive more and experience abundance in every area of my life. I am a faithful, trustworthy, and sensible steward. You can entrust me with additional leadership responsibilities and opportunities, and place me in charge of others. I understand that with great privilege comes great responsibility. For everyone who has been given much, much will be required, and to whom You entrusted much, of that individual, You will ask all the more.

The heaven, the highest heavens, the earth, and everything in it belong to You, God. Because You placed humanity in the Garden of Eden to cultivate and care for it, I can and will exercise dominion, authority, and stewardship in the earth and its resources, always acknowledging Your supreme authority and power. All living creatures, every beast, cattle, bird, and everything that moves, belong to You and must obey me when I speak. I will diligently take care of what You have given me and invest it so I may hear, 'Well done, good and faithful servant. You were faithful with a few things, I will put You in charge of many things; enter into the joy of

Your master." I will not be a wicked, lazy, or unproductive steward. I desire to increase; therefore, I will invest what You have given me so I can receive more and have abundance. I am a faithful, wise, and sensible steward.

Scriptures: Luke 12:42-48; Matt. 25:23; Matt. 25:6; Matt. 25:14-30; Luke 12;48; Deut. 10:14-17; Gen. 2:15-17; Matt. 25:23; 1 Chron. 4:10; Deut. 28:2

Millionaire Confession

The blessing of the Lord brings wealth and makes me rich, and God does not add any sorrow to it. Because I have diligent hands, wealth comes. When I pursue righteousness, prosperity finds me. All my hard work leads to profit. I do not trust in riches. I trust in God. I do not put my hope in wealth, which is so uncertain, but I put my hope in God, who richly provides me with everything for my enjoyment. I avoid debt at all costs. I am a wise person who saves for the future. I invest wisely and prioritize saving money to establish my financial future and achieve long-term security and goals.

I eliminate unnecessary expenses to ensure my financial freedom and avoid debt. I earn extra income from various side jobs, real estate investments, and other ventures. I tithe 10% and save at least 15% of my income. I take advantage of my employer-sponsored 401(k) and 403(b). I also possess Roth IRAs. I seek wise counsel and professional advice for wealth-building strategies when investing. I earn compounding interest on my investments. I have a wealthy mindset. And I am surrounded by other wealthy, affluent, and prosperous people. I am a millionaire.

Scriptures: Prov. 10:22; Prov. 10:4; Prov. 14:23; 1 Tim. 6:17

Guaranteed Financial Security

God will guarantee and safeguard my financial future. He will open up the windows of heaven, the storehouse of His bounty, and send rain on my land in due season and bless all the work of my hands. I will lend to many nations, but will borrow from none. Wisdom is a shelter as money is a shelter, but the advantage of knowledge is that Wisdom preserves those who have it. I do good. I am rich in good deeds. I am generous and willing to share. Thereby, I partake of the treasure laid up for me as a firm foundation for the coming age so that I may take hold of the life that is truly life.

Scriptures: Mal. 3:10; Deut. 15:6; Ecc. 7:12; 1 Tim. 6:18-19

The Power to Get Wealth

The Lord gives me the power to get wealth to establish His covenant on the earth. His blessing makes me rich, wealthy, honored, and favored without adding any sorrow to it. As a result, my house is filled with wealth and riches. My hand is diligent and makes me rich. Pursuing righteousness and love leads to life, prosperity, and honor. Receiving wealth from God is good and a tremendous blessing, and good health to enjoy it is equally valuable. I am incredibly grateful for the ability to enjoy my work and the destiny planned for my life by God, which is a gift from Him. Blessed be the Lord who daily loads me with benefits. Oh, that You would bless me indeed and allow Your favor and blessings to be upon me and overtake me continually!

Scriptures: Deut. 8:17-18; Prov. 10:22; Ps. 112:3; Prov. 10:4; Prov. 21:21; Ecc. 5:19-20; Ps. 68:19

The Blessing of Hard Work

Hard work always pays off. Observe me, because I am good and excel at my job. I am a skilled professional/worker, so I am always consistently in high demand, admired, and highly regarded. I don't take a backseat to anyone. I am the head and not the tail. I am above and never beneath. The LORD my God will bless me in all my endeavors, hard work, and everything I put my hands to. The blessings of the Lord are chasing me down and running me over. He makes everything I do successful.

Scriptures: Prov. 14:23; Prov. 22:29; Deut. 28:12; Deut. 15:10; Ps. 90:17; Deut. 28:2

Generosity

I owe no man anything but to love him. I am debt-free. I am not a slave to the lender. I lend and not borrow. I give generously to others and do so without a reluctant, unwilling, complaining, and resentful heart. The LORD my God will bless all the work of my hands. Because I am righteous, I give generously. God will open to me His wonderful treasury of rain in the heavens so I can have a harvest every season. I give, and it will be given to me: good measure, pressed down, shaken together, and running over will He put into my bosom. With the same measure that I use, it will be measured and returned to me. He will bless everything that I do, and I will lend to many nations but shall not borrow from them.

Scriptures: Rom. 13:8-10; Prov. 22:7; Prov. 11:25; Deut. 28:2; Luke 6:38; Deut. 28:12; Deut. 15:6

Financial Legacy

I am a good person who leaves an inheritance for my children's children. Wealth and riches are in my house. It brims with wealth and a generosity that never runs dry. I am always blessed for doing what is right. Wealth, favor, and glory accompany me, as well as substantial honor and a good name. It endures from generation to generation. When I obey the Lord's commands and walk in His ways, the Lord will establish my family as His holy people. The Lord will increase me more and more, me and my children and my children's children. When the nations of the world see that we are a people claimed by the Lord, they will stand in awe of us.

Scriptures: Prov. 13:22; Ps. 112:3; Prov. 8:18; Deut. 28:9-10; Ps. 115:14-15

The Blessing of the Lord

Even though I am rich, I will not be arrogant nor put my hope in uncertain wealth and riches. My hope is in God, who richly provides me with everything for my enjoyment. The blessing of the Lord makes me rich, and he adds no sorrow to it. I remember the Lord, my God, who gives me the ability to produce wealth. He confirms His covenant, which He swore to my ancestors. And God will generously provide all that I need. He takes care of me and will supply all my needs from His glorious riches, which have been given to me in Christ Jesus.

Scriptures: 1 Tim. 6:17; Prov. 10:22; Deut. 8:18; 2 Cor. 9: 8-15; Phil. 4:19

Supernatural Breakthrough

God, You are the God of the Breakthroughs. You are the Lord, my God, who is faithful, who keeps His covenant, for a thousand generations. You lavish Your unfailing love on me because I love You and obey Your commands. Your faithfulness towards me is why I wait upon You, for Your Word brings me hope, and all of Your promises are yes and amen. Please contend, O Lord, with those who contend with me and fight against those who fight against me. I await Your instruction to pursue, overtake, and without fail, recover all.

My life shines brighter than the noonday because Jesus sits on the throne. You make all things new and are doing a new thing that springs forth a new era of abundance. You make a way in the wilderness by carving paths and creating rivers in the desert. Turn it around in my favor, Lord. It's impossible to please You without unwavering faith and bring You glory. I will not waver at the promise of God through unbelief. I am strengthened in faith, giving You glory. I am thoroughly convinced and fully persuaded that what You have promised You are well able to perform it.

I feel renewed and empowered, ready to emerge again and embrace the fresh start that You have given me. Words are inadequate to express my gratefulness. You rewrote the text of my life when I opened the book of my heart to Your eyes. You gave me a fresh start. I thank You for the new day, the new opportunity, and the spiritual breakthrough. You are definitely the rewarder of those who sincerely, diligently, and earnestly seek You and seek to please You. Your eyes run to and from, roaming throughout the entire earth, seeking to show Yourself strong and demonstrate Your power on behalf of those whose hearts are loyal and faithful to You.

Scripture: Job 1:27; Is. 43:18-19; Rev. 21:5; 2 Chron. 14:11; Ps. 130:5-8; 2 Cor 1:19-20; Heb. 11:6; Ps 18:20-24; 1 Sam. 30:8; Ps. 35:1; Rom. 4:20-21; 2 Chron. 16:9

Harvest

When I walk in Your statutes, keep Your commandments, and perform them, then You will give me rain in its season, the land shall yield its produce, and the trees of the field shall yield their fruit. I will not grow weary while doing good, for in due season I shall reap if I do not lose heart. Whatsoever a man sows, that will he/she surely reap. When I sow sparingly, I reap sparingly; when I sow bountifully, I reap bountifully.

Scriptures: Lev. 26:3-4; Gal. 6:9

Financial Provision

The best is yet to come because I give to other people, and God gives back to me even more than I gave. You fill my pocket until it overflows over the top. I receive good measure, pressed down, shaken together, and running over into my bosom. My simple act of obedience and faith opens up the windows of heaven and ends my financial slavery to the lender. I sow bountifully, and I reap bountifully. I accept a life-changing turnaround in my finances.

Scriptures: Luke 6:38; 2 Cor. 9:6

Exceeding Abundant Blessing

The Lord lavishes me with all good things: children from my womb, offspring from my animals and pets, and crops from my land. God, give me the land that You promised my ancestors that You would give me. Throw open the doors of Your sky vaults, pour out the rain on my land on schedule, and bless the work of my hand so I can lend to many nations and not have to borrow. Make me the head, not the tail, so I am always the top dog, never the underdog. I obediently listen to and diligently keep Your commands, God. I do not swerve an inch to the right or left from the words that You have commanded me.

Scripture: Deut. 28:12

Deciding on the Right Course of Action

Decision Making

Jesus is the same, yesterday, today, and forever. Therefore, I am not unstable, unpredictable, and uncertain in anything I do. I am not tossed back and forth by indecisiveness. I have a clear vision with established goals. I take action quickly and avoid overanalyzing or overthinking my decisions. I do not fear making wrong decisions because God makes my crooked paths straight. My heart is undivided because God teaches and directs me to the right path. I follow the peace of God, which guards my mind against anxiety. I refuse to lean to my own understanding but rather trust in the Lord with all my heart and mind. I am rooted, built up, and strengthened in Christ. Therefore, I am not fickle or worldly in my decision-making. My yes is yes, and my no is no. Because I commit everything I do to the Lord, He establishes my plans and orders my steps. Therefore, I am blessed because I trust in the Lord.

Scriptures: Heb. 13:8; Eph. 4:14; James 1:8; Is. 45:2; Ps. 32:8; Phil. 4:7; Prov. 3:5; Col. 2:7; Eph. 3:17; Matt. 5:37; Ps. 37:5; Prov. 16:3; Ps. 37:23; Jer. 17:7

Wavering Faith

I do not waver in my faith. I am not a double-minded or unstable individual. I am settled in my spirit and not tossed back and forth in my mind. You, Lord, keep me in perfect peace because my mind stays on You. I stand on Your Word and Your promises because You said I have not because I ask not. Your way is always best. I choose to follow You and Your commandments. I stand on the rock-solid foundation of Your Word regardless of the stressors that come my way. You are the anchor for my soul, keeping me stable and secure.

Scriptures: Is. 26:3; 2 Tim. 4:2-5; James 4:2; Ps. 119:173-194; Ps. 26:12; Matt. 7:24-27; Heb. 6:29; Rom. 4:20-22; James 1:9; Ezk. 37:14

Hearing from God

Father, as I enter our secret place, I close my mind to the busyness and craziness of the day so I can hear from You. Speak, Lord, for Your servant hears. I am Your sheep who hears and knows Your voice. You call me by name and lead me where I should go. You said, "You do nothing unless You reveal the secret to Your servants." I am Your servant, Lord, and I will not follow a stranger's voice. I shall not live by bread alone, but by every word that proceeds from the mouth of God. Please show me the new thing You desire to do, so I can perceive it through my senses and obtain understanding and awareness.

Make the crooked path straight and the rough places smooth as You lead me in the paths that I must go. Turn the darkness into light so I can see correctly. I ask You to guide my feet toward peace and help me to be a light to the world. I only need one word from You to change my life. A still, small voice. Confirm Your word to me like You did to Peter. Lord, if it's You, bid me to come to You. Thank you for Your direction, guidance, and wisdom in every area of my life. I immediately act upon what You tell me, so I can experience success in whatever I put my hands to.

Scriptures: Matt. 6:6; 1 Sam. 3:7-11; John 10:27-28; Amos 3:7; John 10:5; Heb. 5:14; Prov. 4:5-9; IS 45:2; Luke 3: 4-6; Luke 1:7-9; Matt. 5:14-16; Matt. 14:29; 1 Kings 19:12; Matt. 4:4

Guidance From the Holy Spirit

Holy Spirit, guide me into all truth. Speak what You hear from the Father, and tell me what is to come. Make it known to me by saying, "This is the way; walk in it." When I call to You, answer me and tell me great and hidden things that I do not know. I belong to You, and I am entitled to hear from You. I am a son/daughter of God. Therefore, I am led by the Spirit of God. When I hear Your voice, I will not harden my heart.

Your words are life-changing. They are living, active, and sharper than any two-edged sword. They judge the thoughts and feelings of my heart. Thank you for Your confident assurance in every step I take. When I call, You answer me and tell me great and hidden things to come. Allow the Holy Spirit to help me remember what You have said and teach me everything, all that You would have me know.

Scriptures: John 16:13; Is. 30:21; Jer. 33:3; Rom. 8:14; Heb. 3:15; Heb. 4:14; 1 John 5:14; John 14:26

Not Leaning to My Own Understanding

Lord, I trust in You with all my heart and lean not on my own understanding. Your word is a lamp for my feet, illuminating my path and providing the light and direction I need. Instruct me and teach me the way I should go. Counsel me with Your loving eye on me. Whether I turn to the right or the left, let my ears confidently hear Your voice behind me, declaring, 'This is the way; walk in it.'

Guide me continually, Lord. Show me Your ways, Lord, teach me Your paths. Father, because I delight in You, make my footsteps firm. I commit to You everything that I do so You can establish my steps and my plans. Your plans are wonderful, and Your wisdom is magnificent beyond measure. Guide me continually with purpose and clarity on a straight path and level ground, leading me to fulfill my remarkable destiny.

Scriptures: Prov. 3:5; Ps. 119:105; Ps. 32:8; Is. 30:21; Is. 58:11; Prov 16:9; Ps. 25:4; Ps. 48:14; Is. 28:29; Ps. 143:10; Ps. 37:23; Prov 16:3; Is. 28:29; Ps. 31:9

Waiting On God

God, unfold Your plan and purpose for my life. Your timing is perfect. I wait for You, Lord. I wait expectantly, and in Your Word do, I hope. Waiting on You, Lord, is not easy. It is immensely challenging. I ask You to give me a promise to hold onto because it helps me manage my expectations and keep the vision before me. I seek direction and wisdom while waiting so that I won't stray from God's will. I know there's a purpose for waiting.

I wait for clear direction as You build my character, resilience, humility, and compassion. You see the end from the beginning. So, I will not rush ahead of You, linger behind You, or step out of Your will. I wait with a great attitude. I do not complain, grumble, or become frustrated with having my own immediate needs, impulses, or desires satisfied. I won't test You, nag You, or forget Your work. Do not grant me my request and then send emptiness into my soul or afflict me with disease or death. Your grace is sufficient for me. Your power is made perfect in my weakness. Your power rests upon me. For when I am weak, then I am strong.

I walk step in step with You with a great attitude. I wait patiently, quietly, and expectantly because I know I will not lose the promise that rightfully belongs to me. My heart will take courage while I wait for the Lord! The Lord is good to those waiting for Him and the soul seeking Him. You shall strengthen my heart, and I will see the goodness of the Lord in the land of the living.

Scriptures: Lam. 3:15; Ps. 130; Ps. 27; 2 Cor. 12:8-10

The Will of God For My Life

For You know the thoughts that You think towards me, thoughts of peace and not of evil; plans for my welfare to give me hope in my final outcome so I can have a flourishing end. You have a specific plan and purpose for my life. I ask You to reveal it to me when I call upon You and pray to You. When I seek You, allow me to find You when I search for You with all my heart. Oh Lord, show me the right path, and point out the road that I should follow. Teach me Your way. Your word is a lamp to guide my feet and a light for my path.

Oh Lord, show me Your purpose, plan, and heart's desires for me. I need Your help because my desires are great. Forgive me for all my past mistakes and for ignoring red flags. I trust You, Lord, to give me peace like an umpire. Quiet any doubts and give me overwhelming peace. Lord, show me what to do. I will listen to You because You have the very best in mind for me. I have many plans in my mind, but Your purpose for me will prevail and stand. Therefore, I surrender my will to You, and I ask that Your perfect will be done in my life. I make the necessary changes and course corrections to please You because Your plans for my life are best for me.

Scriptures: Jer 29: 10-14; Ps. 25:4-9; Ps. 119:105; Prov. 19:21; Matt. 6:9-10

Character Development

I wholeheartedly embrace my new nature. I am designed to reflect God's righteousness and holiness. This transformation makes me a new and different person who is holy and good. I choose to adopt and clothe myself with this new identity. It's a God-inspired life that is renewed from the inside out, and I radiate God's character in every area of my life as I am continually renewed and molded into Christ's image.

A Christ-like character is beneficial and equips me to navigate life's challenges and adversity. The trials I face and the testing of my faith will cultivate endurance, steadfastness, and patience, which are cornerstones for character development. This endurance fosters spiritual maturity and inner peace, leading to a thorough transformation in my life. It produces a better version of me, and I emerge perfect and complete in my faith, lacking nothing, improving my relationships and influence in this world.

Every action I take should resonate with God's glory. When I allow my light to shine through my good character, I invite the world to see my good works and glorify my Father in heaven. Good character leads to honor, respect, love, joy, peace, patience, kindness, goodness, faithfulness, and, most importantly, a good name. Embracing these qualities will illuminate my path and ensure that I leave a meaningful and lasting legacy.

Scriptures: Eph. 4:24; James 1:2-4; 1 Cor. 10:31; Prov. 22:1; Prov. 3:5-6; John 15:8

Career Choices

Father, I find myself in need of wisdom, and I know You give generously to anyone who asks. I am unsure of the path that I need to take in life. You desire to prosper me, and You have an excellent plan for my life. Please reveal that plan so I can follow it. I acknowledge that I am Your workmanship, a masterpiece created with specific gifts, talents, abilities, passions, and personality. While my heart plans my ways, You establish my steps. Give me direction and purpose.

I seek Your support in making an informed decision. Surround me with the right advisors so my plans can succeed. I understand the importance of seeking wise counsel, as plans often fail without it. Instruct me and teach me the way I should go, keeping Your watchful eye upon me. Help me find fulfillment in my career choice. Keep me free from the love of money so that I can prioritize my passion, contentment, and work-life balance over stress and long sleepless nights. I want to make a meaningful difference and impact in the world that draws others closer to You.

Scriptures: James 1:5-8; Prov. 3:6; Jer. 29:11; Eph. 2:10; Prov. 16:9; Prov. 11:4; Ps. 32:8; Prov. 5:21; Prov. 15:3; Heb. 13:5

Purchasing Land/Building A Home

Someone builds every house, but God is the builder of everything. God, please build my house so my labor is not in vain. I want my house to be built upon a rock-solid foundation. I need Your direction in choosing the right location and neighborhood to build or purchase my home. I desire a safe neighborhood where kids can play and run freely and safely. I ask for my family's protection from the presence of pedophiles, drug dealers, domestic violence abusers, and sex offenders residing in my neighborhood. My neighbors are respectful. They clean up after their pets, avoid playing loud music, and parking improperly in other people's driveways. I envision well-maintained yards free from junk or abandoned vehicles. You are a God of order, and You consistently remind me that evil company corrupts good habits.

Help me expand my vision to include more peaceful dwelling places, secure homes, and tranquil spaces for rest in my neighborhood. This represents the quality of life that You desire for Your chosen people. Stretch my faith to see beyond my current situation. I desire a safe neighborhood with excellent schools, parks, playgrounds, walkable communities, the ability to age in place, and the correct number of bedrooms and bathrooms. By wisdom, a house is built, and through understanding, it is established. With knowledge, its rooms are filled with rare and beautiful treasures. Order my footsteps so I can reside in peaceful places that promote a good, fulfilling quality of life.

As I prepare, I commit to changing my mindset to embrace saving over splurging. Empower me to start strong, stay focused, and finish well. Thank you for providing the financial resources that increase my buying power. I carefully consider and estimate the cost of building and/or purchasing this property. God, You delight in the prosperity of Your servant, so please send the necessary finances to build or buy this property. The plans of the diligent lead to profit. Help me to look ahead, maintain a clear vision, and exercise self-discipline as I prepare to purchase land or a new home.

Scriptures: Heb. 3: 4; Matt. 7:24-27; Ps. 127; Prov. 21:5; 1 Cor. 15:33; Luke 14:28-30; Ps. 37:23, Heb. 6:12; Prov. 13:20; Is. 32:18; Prov. 24:3-6.

Timing is Everything

There is an appointed time for everything. And there is a time for every event under heaven. What may seem like an eternity to me it's only a day to You, Lord. I do not tire or give up because I will reap a harvest of blessings if I do not give up, persevere, and do not lose heart. There is a right time and a right way to do everything.

Please assist me in making major life decisions such as choosing the right person and the right time to marry, deciding when to have a child/children, making career decisions, considering relocations, pursuing educational endeavors, and making large and small purchases like a home, car, renovations, furniture, etc., My times are in Your hands, and I trust that You will make everything work together for my good. While I may not know the times or seasons of Your timetable or understand it, I entrust You with my life.

Scriptures: Acts 1:7; Ps. 31:15; Rom. 8:28; Ecc. 8:6; Ecc. 3:1; 2 Pet. 3:8; Gal. 6:9; Ecc. 8:9

Trusting God While Waiting

Lord, I entrust my life to Your hands. I place my trust in You, knowing that I will not be disappointed. My enemies will not laugh at me, for no one who trusts in You will be disappointed. I cast all my cares, all anxieties, all worries, and all concerns upon You once and for all. You care about me with the deepest affection and watch over me very carefully and attentively. I am confident that You will save me, and I wait patiently for You to answer my prayers.

I do not take matters into my own hands. You make everything happen at the right time. However, the time approaches when the vision will be fulfilled slowly, steadily, and surely. Therefore, I will not despair at how long this is taking, for my request will surely come to pass. I refuse to be anxious or worried about anything. Instead, through prayer and petition with thanksgiving, I continue to make my specific requests known to You in every circumstance and situation.

I will exercise patience because it will not be overdue a single day! The peace of God, which reassures my heart, transcends all understanding and stands guard over my heart and mind in Christ Jesus. I maintain a tranquil state within my soul. I have waited patiently for You, Lord, and You leaned toward me and heard my cry. At the right time, You, Lord, made it happen. You brought me out of a horrible pit and the muddy clay. You set my feet upon a rock, established my steps, and put a new song in my mouth. I praise and trust in You, Lord.

Scriptures: Ps. 25:1-3; Ps. 40:1-3; Phil. 4:6-7; 1 Pet. 5:7; Is 60:22; Ecc. 3:11; Micah 7:7; Ps. 37:7; Hab. 2:3.

Move Forward

Father, You have bestowed upon me a vision, and I hold that promise before You, reminding You of Your faithfulness. You have inspired me with a powerful word, and You sent others to confirm it, igniting a fire in my heart. Yet, I struggle with discouragement due to the delays and inaction I see. Still, I choose to praise, pray, and push ahead, regardless of my feelings or circumstances. This is the day that the Lord has made, and I will rejoice in it with all my heart.

Father, empower and equip me to run this race with perseverance, shedding anything that may hinder my progress. Help me to move forward and keep my gaze fixed on the incredible new things You have in store for me in my life. Grant me strength and amplify my power. Your vision is set for an appointed time, and in the end, it will undoubtedly manifest. Though it may seem delayed, I will wait with unwavering anticipation, knowing it is on the way.

Thank you for empowering the weak and renewing my strength as I wait on You. I am ready to spread my wings and soar like an eagle. I run and do not grow weary; I walk and do not falter. I will not fall behind in any aspect of my journey.

Scriptures: Heb. 12:1-2; Is. 43:18-19; Is. 40:29-31

Discerning Truth From Error And Right From Wrong

The Gift of Discernment

Thank you for the gift of discernment and a listening heart. As Your servant, I have an understanding mind that discerns between good and evil and distinguishes Your character and will in every circumstance. I have an understanding heart that despises what is evil and embraces what is good. I possess a mindset rooted in Your word, which enables me to decisively test and scrutinize the spirits, distinguishing between what is from You and what is not and confidently discerning right from wrong.

I see as You see. Therefore, I do not judge others solely by their outward appearances but consider the individual's heart. I discern the thoughts and intentions of the heart. As I mature in Your Word, I continually practice distinguishing between good and evil so that I may not call evil good and good evil. I live an uncompromising life pleasing to You. Let Your voice ring loudly in my ears.

Scriptures: 1 Cor. 12: 8-10; 1 John 4:1-3; Heb. 5:14; Heb. 4:12; 1 Kings 3:9; Is. 5:20

The Spirit of Discernment

The Spirit of God within me makes me discerning and wise. He opens doors that no man can shut. He opens doors that allow God to be glorified. The Spirit of God allows favor to flourish in my life. I am Your servant; give me discernment that I may understand Your statutes. Give me the wisdom to govern Your people. Teach me how to exercise sound judgment and knowledge. Teach me to do Your will. Help me to test the spirits and rightfully divide the Word. I recognize lying spirits, deception, dishonesty, and other ungodly words and actions in others. Your prayer for me is that my love may abound more and more in knowledge and depth of insight so that I may be able to discern what is best and may be pure and blameless for the day of Christ.

I eat solid food, and I am of full age. I exercise my senses to discern both good and evil. I do not conform to the pattern of this world, but I am transformed by the renewing of my mind daily. I am able to test and approve what God's will is—His good, pleasing, and perfect will. All knowledge begins with fear and respect for the Lord. He gives wisdom and understanding of vision and dreams. Teach me to do Your will, for You are my God. May Your good Spirit lead me on level ground so I can acquire knowledge and seek it out as people do. The Advocate, the Holy Spirit, teaches me all things and reminds me of everything the Word of God says.

Scriptures: 1 Cor. 3:16; Rom. 8:9; 1 John 4:4; Rev. 3:8; Ps. 119:125; 1 Kings 3:9; Ps. 143:10; 2 Tim. 2:15; Phil 1:9-11; Heb. 5:14; Rom. 12:2; Dan. 1:17; Ps. 143:10; John 14:26

Spiritual Wisdom

I make a special request. Fill me with the full, deep, and clear knowledge of Your will in all spiritual wisdom, in comprehensive insight into the ways and purposes of God, and in understanding and discernment of spiritual things. I want to walk (live and conduct myself) in a manner worthy of the Lord, fully pleasing to Him. I desire to please Him in all things, bearing fruit in every good work and steadily growing and increasing in and by the knowledge of God [with fuller, deeper, and clearer insight, acquaintance, and recognition].

Scriptures: Col. 1:9-10

Speak to My Heart, Lord

In the beginning was the Word, and the Word was with God, and the Word was God. Father, You said to call to You and that You would answer me and reveal great and mighty things that I have not known, have knowledge of, and understand. Speak to my heart, Lord. Your servant listens. I need a divine word from You. If I can hear from You, I'll know what to do. I am Your sheep who longs to hear Your voice and follow You because You give me eternal life to avoid a perishing predicament.

The Word of God is living and active, sharper than any two-edged sword, piercing and penetrating deep into the division of my soul and spirit, of joints and of marrow, and discerning the thoughts and intentions of the heart. Your scripture is invaluable and profitable for teaching, reproof, correction, and training in righteousness. Your Word never returns void back to You but fulfills and accomplishes that which You purpose and succeeds in the task, that thing for which You sent it. Because I hear Your Word, I am like a wise person who built my home on a solid rock foundation.

Scriptures: Jer. 33:3; John 10:27-28; Heb. 4:12; 2 Tim 3:16; Is: 55:11; Matt 7:24; John 1:1; 1 Sam. 3:7-11

Revelation

The word of God is living and active, dynamic and powerful, sharper than any two-edged sword, piercing into the very core and division of my soul and spirit, of my joints and marrow, and discerning my thoughts and the intentions of my heart. My faith is ignited from hearing and hearing the word of God. Father, when You speak, help me to perceive it and grant me the wisdom to understand it. As I abide and remain in You, empower me to bear much fruit abundantly. Guide me into all truth so that I will speak and do whatever I hear. My words and actions align with Your will.

Unveil the future. Declare to me the things that are to come. Allow the Holy Spirit to teach me all things and bring to my remembrance all You have said. You promised, "Whatever I ask for in prayer, believe that I have received it, and it will be mine." Lord, I call upon You for help in my distress and times of trouble. Hear my voice from Your sanctuary, and let my cry reach and resonate in Your ears.

The Lord is near and close to all who call on Him, to all who call on Him in truth and sincerity. You fulfill the desire of those who fear You. Hear my cry, O Lord, and save me. Rescue me, Lord. As a child of God, I am guided by the Spirit of God. When I hear Your voice, I will follow You faithfully.

Scriptures: Rom 10:17; Job 33:14; John 15:1-27; John 16:13; John 14:16; Ps. 18:6; Ps. 145:18-19; John 6:63

Avoiding Naïve Decision Making

The naïve believes everything, but a sensible person carefully considers their steps. Therefore, I wholeheartedly embrace knowledge and avoid making hasty decisions that could lead to foolish, stupid, careless, avoidable, and regrettable mistakes. I am diligent in everything that I do. It's my guiding principle to make intentional decisions and plans that give me the advantage and lead me to favorable outcomes. I seek the advice and counsel of others so my plans are fruitful and not frustrating. The Lord will help me not to be naïve. He grants me wisdom, favor, and grace. He will not punish me for making an unwise decision because His grace and mercy abound. He will also spare me the consequences of making foolish decisions. I believe that my faithfulness brings blessings into my life.

Scriptures: Prov. 14:15; Prov. 28:25; Prov. 11:14

The Benefits of Wisdom

God generously gives wisdom to anyone who asks Him for it if they lack it. I am blessed when I find wisdom and gain understanding. I listen to advice and accept discipline so I can be considered and counted among the wise. The Wisdom that comes from heaven is pure, peace-loving, considerate, submissive, full of mercy, bearing good fruit, impartial, and sincere. I will never forsake Wisdom because she shields and protects me, and I love her because she watches over me. Obtaining Wisdom is a worthy and crucial pursuit. I develop common sense, good judgment, discernment, comprehension, interpretation, and wisdom. I am wise and act justly. Acquiring wisdom is costly, but it is so worth the investment. The one who gains wisdom loves life. Those who cherish understanding will soon prosper and thrive. Wisdom is better than gold and silver. Wisdom and understanding are evident in my good life and my humble deeds. Because I please God, He grants me wisdom, knowledge, and happiness.

Scriptures: James 1:5; Prov. 19:20; Ecc. 7:12; Prov. 3:13-18; Prov. 4:7; James 3:17; Ecc. 1:14

Choosing the Right Alliances

I soar with eagles because I am righteous. I choose my friends carefully and with discernment. They help me to be strong in the Lord and to put on the whole armor of God. We encourage one another and build each other up. My intercessor is my friend as my eyes pour out tears to God. When I pray for my friends, the Lord will restore their fortunes and give them double for their trouble. My alliances do not lead me astray or mislead me, as bad company corrupts good character. My company possesses good character.

They help me when I fall, and I do the same for them. We have each other's backs. My alliances are consistent and reliable. They stick closer than a brother or a sister, offering unwavering support. They give me pleasant and heartfelt advice. We love each other as Christ first loved us. We love at all times. Greater love has no one than this: to lay down one's life for one's friends. My friends are not hot-tempered. I do not associate with individuals who are easily angered. I refuse to be entrapped and snared by the devil. I am like Jesus and do what He commands me. Jesus is my friend, and everything he has learned from His Father, God, He has graciously made known to me.

Scriptures: 1 Cor. 15:33; Is. 40:31; Eph. 6:10; Job 16:20-21; 1 Thess. 5:11; Prov. 18:24; 1 John 4:19; Prov. 17:17; John 15:13; Prov. 22:24; 2 Tim. 2:26; 1 John 3:2; John 15:15

Healthy Friendships

Iron sharpens iron. I am grateful for my healthy friendships and relationships. I appreciate those who celebrate me and bring joy into my life. My friends inspire me to improve and refuse to let me settle in my comfort zone or misery. Their encouragement empowers me to think bigger and better than I currently do about my circumstances and situation. With their unwavering optimism and kindness, they enrich my life without a trace of envy for what I have. Their tranquil hearts are a source of strength and vitality for me. Their peaceful hearts give me life. I recognize that envy and jealousy lead to decay; they breed disorder and every vile practice. I am committed to discerning between true, genuine friends and those who use me or measure themselves against me for their own gain. I seek to grow in wisdom, stature, and favor with both God and man. Love is my foundation—a seal upon my heart and Your arm—because love is as strong as death, while jealousy only brings destruction. Its flames are fierce, like the very fire of the Lord, and I embrace the powerful energy of true friendship.

Scriptures: Is. 30:21; Prov. 14:30; Luke 2:52; Song 8:6; Exo. 20:17; James 3:13-16; Exo. 20:17

Order My Footsteps

The end of a thing is better than its beginning. The Lord instructs you and teaches you in the way you should go. He counsels me with His loving eye. Show me Your ways, LORD, teach me Your paths. And when I turn to the right or when I turn to the left, my ears shall hear a word behind me, saying, 'This is the way; walk in it.' I commit my work to the Lord, and my plans will be established. God knows the plans He has for me: plans to prosper me and not to harm me, plans to give me a hope and a future. God has determined my pre-appointed times and the boundaries of my dwelling.

Scriptures: Ecc. 7:8; Ps. 32:8; Ps. 25:4-5; Is. 30:21; Prov. 16:3; Jer. 29:11; Acts. 17:26

Obedience

I am passionately devoted to God with all my heart, soul, and might. I am a doer of the word and not a hearer only. This Book of the Law shall not depart from my mouth, but I shall meditate on it day and night to carefully ensure that I do everything written in it. My obedience and meditation in the word of God pave the way for my prosperity and ensure good success.

When I obey God's commandments, I remain in His love, just as Jesus obeyed His Father's commandments and remained in His love. Obedience fills me with joy, and my joy overflows! Because of my obedience, God will indeed bless me and my descendants abundantly. I am strong and incredibly courageous, meticulously following everything written in the Word of God. I do not stray, wander, or drift to the right hand or the left, so I can have good success wherever I go and in everything I do.

Scriptures: Deut. 6:4-9; James 1:22-25; Josh. 1:8; John 15:9-12; Gen. 22:19; Josh. 1:7

Cultivating a Spirit of Humility

Lord, You delight in Your people and crown the humble with victory. When I embrace and clothe myself with humility, You show me favor. I do nothing from selfish ambition or conceit but humbly count and value others more significant than myself. I put the interests of others ahead of my own, just like Christ did. I have the mind of Christ. I empty myself and become a servant to all.

I do not think of myself more highly than I should, but I think of myself with sober judgment. I do nothing out of selfish ambition or vain conceit. But instead, in humility, I value others above myself. I will not praise myself but let others praise me.

Pride brings disgrace, and humility brings wisdom. I choose to walk humbly with You, knowing that You will elevate me when I humble myself before You. You guide the humble in what is right and teach them Your way. Humility is the fear of the Lord; its rewards are riches, honor, and life. I cultivate a spirit of humility because it is pleasing to You.

Scriptures: Ps. 149:4; Phil. 2:3; 1 Cor. 2:16; Rom. 12:3; Prov. 11:21; James 4:10; Ps. 25:9; Prov. 22:4-5

Persistent Confident Prayer

Father, I earnestly pray for Your will to be done on earth as it is in heaven. I devote myself to prayer with a clear and alert mind and a grateful heart. I enter Your gates with thanksgiving and Your courts with praise, giving thanks and praise to Your holy name. Because You have limited Your authority on the earth, I exercise dominion and authority on the earth. Let the demonstration of Your spirit and power follow me. Whatever I bind on earth shall be bound in heaven, and whatever I loose on earth shall be loosed in heaven. I expect Your power and anointing to manifest greatly. I speak the word of God in faith and power, knowing it brings results and answers.

Scriptures: Ps. 100:4; Col. 4:2; Matt. 6:10; Matt. 18:18

Filled with All Knowledge, Spiritual Wisdom, and Understanding

Father, fill me with the knowledge of Your will in all spiritual wisdom and understanding so that I may walk in a manner worthy of You, Lord, pleasing You in all respects, bearing fruit in every good work, and increasing the knowledge of God. I am strengthened with all power, according to Your glorious might, for the attaining of all steadfastness and patience; joyously giving thanks to the Father, who has qualified me to share in the inheritance of the saints in light.

Scriptures: Col. 1:9-12

Delay in Answered Prayer

I will not be afraid, for from the first day I set my heart on understanding and humbling myself before God, You heard my prayer, and a heavenly angel came to respond to my request. Your promises are yes and amen. I understand that my struggle is not against flesh and blood but against the rulers, the authorities, the powers of this dark world, and the spiritual forces of evil in the heavenly realms. Forgive me of my sins.

Thank you for not answering my prayers if I pray amiss and improperly for anything that is harmful and detrimental to myself and others. I know that Your timing is perfect. Help me wait patiently for Your perfect timing as You arrange everything for my benefit. While waiting on You, God, help me set my house in order so that I am equipped and prepared to receive my request. I know that I win regardless of how long it takes. I strengthen myself in Your word. I refuse to be anxious, knowing that the peace of God will guard my heart and mind in Christ Jesus.

Scriptures: Eph. 6:12; Dan. 10:12-13; Phil. 4:6-7

Discerning the Will of God

As I continue to grow and mature in my faith, anoint me, Father, with the garment of spiritual discernment. This precious gift will transform me when fully realized, empowering me to distinguish between good and evil, truth and deception, and wisdom and falsehood. Grant me an understanding mind to govern Your people, that I may discern between good and evil. Enable me to distinguish between manipulations and deceptions so that I won't believe every spirit but instead test the spirits to see whether they are of You or not.

Let my love abound more and more, with knowledge and all discernment, so that You may approve what is excellent and be found pure and blameless for the day of Christ. The Word of God is living and active, sharper than any two-edged sword, piercing to the division of soul and spirit, of joints and marrow, and discerning the thoughts and intentions of the heart. I refuse to conform to this world. I am transformed through the renewal of my mind, a process guided by discernment and wisdom.

Through testing, I seek to discern God's will and what is good, acceptable, and perfect, thereby committing myself to spiritual growth.

Recognizing my lack of wisdom, I turn to God, who gives generously to all without reproach. I ask for the wisdom to discern between spirits. The natural person does not accept the things of the Spirit of God, for they are folly to him, and he cannot understand them because he must discern them in the Spirit. I do not judge by appearances. I judge with the proper judgment. You are sending me out as a sheep among wolves, so equip me to be as wise as a serpent and as innocent as a dove. To whom much is given, much is required. Guide me in cultivating wisdom and embracing vulnerability so that I may effectively fulfill Your purpose for me on earth.

Scripture: 1 John 4:1; Heb. 5:14; Phil. 1:9-10; Heb. 4:12; 1 King 3:9; Rom. 12:2; James 1:5; 1 Cor. 2:14; John 7:24; Matt. 10:16; 1 Cor. 12:10; Luke 12:48

Blessings Upon Blessings

World Changer Leadership

I am a servant of the Most-High God. I wash the feet of others. I do nothing out of selfish ambition or vain conceit. Rather, in humility, I value others above myself and prioritize and focus on their interests. I can do all things through Him, who gives me strength. Everything I do flows from my heart, so I must guard it. Because I have an excellent spirit within me, I am skilled in my work, and therefore, I serve before high-ranking officials and kings. I remain above reproach, faithful to my spouse, pleasant, self-controlled, respectable, and hospitable. My speech and my conduct serve as an example for others. I walk in love, exercising faith and purity. I am kind, welcoming, friendly, sociable, and generous. I remain blameless and self-controlled.

I am not overbearing, quick-tempered, violent, or given to dishonest gain. I commit my way to the LORD, trust in Him, and He makes it come to pass. I encourage others and avoid meaningless talk, deception, and dishonest gain. Arrogance, pride, and selfishness are far from me. I look to the Lord, who is my help, and gives me hinds' feet over all my places of responsibility and trouble. The Lord refreshes me when I am tired so I can continue to do good and not lose my harvest of blessings. I refuse to be intimidated by their faces or afraid of doing what is right in this leadership role. God is with me. So, whom shall I fear? I will not be discouraged because God is with me. He strengthens and helps me. He upholds me with His victorious, righteous right hand.

Scriptures: Acts 16:17; John 13:14-15; Phil 2:3-4; Phil. 4:13; Prov. 4:23; Dan. 5:12; Prov. 22:29; 1 Tim 3:2; Col. 3:12-14; Titus 1:7; Ps. 37:5; Is. 65:24; Ps. 121:1-2; Heb. 3:19; Jer. 31:25; Phil. 1:28; Ps. 27:1-2; Is. 41:10

Anointing

Father, I put You in remembrance of Your word. You said, "whatever things I ask when I pray, believe that I receive them, and I will have them." I pray that You will give me an immeasurable, unusual anointing where signs and wonders follow. May God's anointing dwell, abide in me, and guide and teach me about all things in Jesus' name. This anointing empowers me to spread the gospel of the Lord Jesus Christ. It sets captives free, opens blind eyes, and deaf ears. It delivers the oppressed in Jesus' name, and heals the sick with the laying on of hands. This anointing helps me to powerfully fulfill the purpose, the tasks, and the assignments You have given me. I seek this anointing for myself and my children. Set us apart for Your purpose in Jesus' name. Father, pour Your oil on me and use me mightily so I can boldly fulfill Your dominion mandate on the earth and bring glory to Your name.

Scriptures: Is. 43:26; Mark 11:24; Mark 16:20; John 14:26; Luke 4:18; Mark 16:18; Rom. 12:1-2

Bearing Fruit/Equipped For Success

Jesus, You are the vine. I am the branches. When I abide in You, You abide in me and cause me to bear much fruit. You chose, appointed and purposefully placed, and planted me so that I would go and bear fruit and keep on bearing, and that my fruit would remain and be lasting. Because You are with me, I am strong. I draw strength from You because I am deeply rooted in You, which increases my anointing and empowers me to prosper. Because You are in me, I am nourished in my spirit and my soul, which leads and promotes my growth and increases my health.

Because I am connected to You, I am guaranteed protection from the elements and things that would seek to destroy me. I am led by the Holy Spirit daily. I remain firmly established, secure, immovable, stable, steadfast, and firm in my commitment to You. I refuse to waver. You are my safe haven who calms and soothes me against the overwhelming stressors of life. Your divine presence is my refuge and my hiding place that permits me to flourish, be fruitful, and multiply. Now, I draw upon that peaceful environment. Transform my life and my home into a stress-free oasis. Have Your way in my life, Lord. I need You more than ever before.

Scriptures: John 15: 1-20;1 Cor. 15:58; Ps. 45:2; Ps. 91:2

Business Success

Continually, I set God's word before me to increase my knowledge and understanding. I have written the vision and made it plain. I presented my business plans before the Lord, so that everything would go well. I am led and guided by the Holy Spirit daily in my business decisions. I navigate the ups and downs of business using godly wisdom.

I serve a niche market, and people desire the products and services I offer. Word of mouth about my business and products increases foot traffic to my store or website. I deliver a consistent product that increases trust, credibility, and sales. My customer service sets my business apart from all my competitors, giving me a competitive edge and advantage.

Opportunities are chasing me down. I am sensitive to fluctuations in the marketplace, and therefore, I pivot quickly. I possess a spirit of excellence in everything that I do. I defy all statistics regarding the demise of my business. As I focus on my business goals, objectives, and purposes, I work diligently and make essential sacrifices to ensure the longevity of my business.

I have a competitive advantage because God is my secret and silent business partner. Regardless of the ups and downs of business, I commit to tithing on all profits made and sowing to advance the kingdom of God. I am diligent, and therefore, I am made rich. I am willing and obedient, and I eat the good of the land. Lastly, I commit everything to the Lord, and He gives me success. I do everything decently and in order, and God makes it happen for me.

Scriptures: Ps. 116:8; Josh. 1:8; Rom. 8:14; Dan. 6:3; Prov. 3:9; Mal. 3:10; Gal. 6:7; Prov. 13:4; Is. 1:19; Prov. 16:3; 1 Cor. 14:40

Marketplace Ministry Anointing

I carry a powerful marketplace anointing that brings transformative results. The Spirit of God is at work within me. God endows me with wisdom, ability, understanding, intelligence, knowledge, and excellence in every aspect of my work (Exo. 31:1-6). These qualities yield a bountiful harvest that enriches and uplifts my church, my business, my partnerships, and my family. I am truly anointed to excel. God's wisdom grants me supernatural insight to resolve problems, difficulties, and challenges.

I introduce witty ideas, innovations, and inventions that make a meaningful difference and impact on the lives of others. My unique gifts and talents create opportunities for me, open doors, and brings me before influential people (Prov. 18:16). I have a good name and maintain a strong reputation. Integrity is my business standard and my calling card. My sphere of influence extends beyond the physical four walls of my business, encompassing my philanthropic and religious activities. Favor surrounds me like a protective shield; people continually use their power, influence, ability, and resources on my behalf. My strong and solid reputation leads to lucrative business deals and investments, resulting in increased profits, customer loyalty, growth, and market presence. In moments where I may not feel naturally qualified, I boldly declare supernatural qualification and anointing for every task I undertake.

I am resolute about my purpose in the marketplace. As salt and light, I create and set my business environment, cultivating an atmosphere filled with prayer, Christian music, and faith-based television programming so that people can feel and perceive the tangible presence of Jesus. I exercise wisdom and discernment as I strategically engage in winning souls for the kingdom. The gifts of the Spirit manifest as needed to minister to my clients and customers, enabling profound transformational impact in their lives as I reclaim territory for Christ in the marketplace.

Scriptures: 1 Cor. 3:16; Exo. 31:1-6; Prov. 18:16; Prov. 22:1; Ps. 5:12; Matt. 5:13; Prov. 4;5; Heb. 5:14; Rom. 12: 4-8

Starting A Successful Business

I want to start a business to address a specific need or explore the option of opening a franchise. I need help choosing the perfect name, website domain, and tagline for my venture. Additionally, I need guidance on selecting a prime location with the right demographics to appeal to a diverse customer base. Please provide me with a roadmap and an actionable business plan to guide me through every aspect of the business. Please provide me with the right guidance and counselors to assist me with the correct business design, development, structure, logistics, marketing strategies, location, and competitive analysis.

Guide me with the business structure to minimize taxes and my personal liability. Please provide the necessary support to assist me with registering the business, obtaining an Employer Identification Number (EIN), acquiring federal and state tax IDs, and securing any essential business licenses and permits. I am seeking a bank account that yields significant interest and dividends. A bank that helps me quickly manage the business's day-to-day activities, such as cash deposits, cash-back reward cards, and convenient ATM locations, to help me manage my expenses and budgeting effectively.

Please provide me with the right strategies for managing finances effectively. I am eager for witty ideas and inventions that lead to the development of products and services that target and resonate with the correct customer base. Send the right personnel who will embrace my vision and dreams, and connect with customers, to create a memorable first impression. I need Your assistance in discerning the right people to hire.

Help me adapt and refine my business approaches to meet product demand and ensure that inventory sells quickly. God, whether it's a brick-and-mortar location, a home office, or an online enterprise, allow my business to flourish and prosper. By providing excellent customer service and high-quality products, I garner rave reviews that generate additional sales, creating free marketing opportunities and advertising through word of mouth and social media platforms.

Failure is not an option. You are my anchor and my silent business partner. I am committed to following Your success principles. My business will glorify and celebrate You eternally.

Scriptures: Ps. 62:6; Heb. 6:19-20; Prov. 16:3

Managing Business Growth

I need Your wisdom in preparing for and managing rapid business growth. Because You are with me, business success overtakes me swiftly. It happens so fast that my head will spin. My hard work, coupled with Your wisdom and discernment, brings a profit. Help me maintain balance, avoiding the tendency to work from morning to evening, as it can jeopardize my health and lead to exhaustion, sleep deprivation, stress, strained family relationships, and fatigue. I seek Your assistance in identifying and selecting capable individuals who fear God, are trustworthy, and are committed to avoiding dishonest gain.

I delegate various tasks, roles, and responsibilities so they can support me in managing the business effectively. These individuals also help me stay competitive by identifying trends and exploring new markets. Based on their insights and by studying market trends, I expand my product lines and services and consider acquiring additional businesses. I am wise, proactive, and vigilant, continually looking ahead so I am not caught off guard.

God, I am grateful for Your support and the power You give me to gain wealth and establish Your covenant. I am equipped and empowered with everything I need to manage the successful growth of my business with prosperity and without scandal. Praise the Lord! Hallelujah!!!!

Scriptures: Prov. 14:23; Prov. 13:8; Deut. 8:18; Amos 9:13; Prov. 28:14; Exo. 18:21; Prov. 14:8; Deut. 8:18

Surrounded by Favor

Favor surrounds me like a shield and lasts for a lifetime. People use their power and their influence on my behalf. You bestow favor and honor upon me. Therefore, You do not withhold any good thing from me because I walk blameless before You. Your favor rests upon me, and You establish the works of my hands. Because people are pleased with my work, I earn favor. Wisdom and favor result in my promotion, preferential treatment, and special advantages. You show favor to the humble. I do not forget Your teaching, and I keep Your commandments in my heart because they prolong my life for many years and bring me peace and prosperity.

Love and faithfulness will never leave me. I bind them around my neck and write them on the tablet of my heart. Therefore, I win favor and a good name in the sight of God and men. God's favor rests upon my life. I find favor in Your sight and with men daily. The time of God's favor is for me and everything and everyone attached to me now.

Favor pursues and overtakes me. The time to favor me is now. The set time has come. I found favor in Your sight, and You do not pass me by. I find favor in the sight of all who look upon me, favor and good understanding in the sight of God and man. May the favor of the Lord our God rest on me; establish the work of my hands.

Scriptures: Ps. 5:12; Prov. 3:27; Gen. 17:1; Ps. 90:17; Prov. 3:1-6

Blessings For The Righteous/Favor

Surely, LORD, You bless the righteous. Daily, You load me with benefits and surround me with a shield of favor, goodwill, and pleasure. I never let love and faithfulness leave me. I bind them around my neck and write them on the tablet of my heart so I can win favor and a good name in the sight of God and man. Let Your favor rest upon me and establish the work of my hands. For You, Lord, are my sun and shield. You are the Lord who bestows favor and honor. No good thing will You withhold from those who walk uprightly and blameless before You.

Scriptures: Ps. 90:17; Ps. 84:11; Ps. 68:19, Prov. 3:3-4; Ps. 5:12

Chosen Instrument Pursuing Purpose

Lord, You made me a chosen instrument to carry Your gospel worldwide. I am a willing vessel. I will not put my hand to the plow and look back. I will not turn back. Nor will I love my father or mother, my son or daughter, more than the Lord. Just as Elisha left everything behind to serve You, I make a permanent decision to walk away from life as I know it completely.

I say goodbye to my occupation, family, and guaranteed financial security to serve You and pursue my purpose. I am fully committed to the kingdom of God. I am all in; one hundred percent committed to picking up my cross and following You. I pray that Your anointing will rest upon me just like it did with Elisha, along with signs, wonders, and miracles that confirm Your presence is with me.

Scriptures: Acts 9:15; 2 Tim. 2:2; Luke 14:26; 1 Kings 19:20-21; Matt. 16:24-26; 2 Kings 2:14; 2 Kings 3:16-25; 2 Kings 5; 2 Kings 6; 2 Kings 8:7-15; 2 Kings 13:14-19

Chosen and Handpicked by God

I am the apple of Your eye. Your face shines upon me as Your prized possession. You have permanently tattooed my name on the palm of Your hand and numbered the hairs on my head. You long to be good to me and validate me daily. You decided to open the windows of heaven and pour out a blessing that I don't have room enough to receive. You chose me and appointed me so that I might go and bear fruit that lasts.

As Your beloved chosen one, I must apply and produce holiness, compassion, kindness, humility, meekness, and patience, and become blameless in Your sight. Before creating the world, You chose me as a special treasure above all the people on the face of the earth. You love me with everlasting love and have drawn me to You with Your unfailing kindness. I am forever grateful, and I will never reject You.

Scriptures: John 15:16; Col. 3:12; Deut. 7:6; Jer. 31:3; Ps. 17:8; Deut. 14:2; Is. 49:16; Luke 12:7; Mal. 3:10

Promotion

I humbly acknowledge that promotion does not come from the East or West. It only comes from God. So, I humble myself in Your presence, Lord, and ask that You exalt me, lift me up, and make my life significant. In everything I do, regardless of the task, I strive to give my very best effort. I consistently always do my best, going above and beyond to please only You. I work from my heart for You, God, knowing You are the one I serve.

I am at Your service, Lord. I humble myself under Your mighty hand, knowing that You will lift me up at the proper time. Place Your strong hand upon me, promote me, and fulfill Your purpose towards me. God, do superabundantly above, more than all that I can dare ask or think, infinitely beyond my greatest prayers, hopes, and dreams, according to Your power that is at work within me. And I will be forever grateful.

Scriptures: Ps. 75:6-7; James 4:10; Eph. 3:20; 1 Pet. 5:6; Col. 3:23

Victorious life

Victory is mine through Christ, who loves me. With the Lord, my God, by my side, I am empowered to triumph over my enemies and all challenges. The Lord, my God, goes with me to fight against my enemies and give me victory regardless of the trouble and tribulations that come my way. I take heart and courage, knowing that He has overcome the world. The eyes of the Lord search the entire earth, ready to display His strength for those wholeheartedly committed to Him. I am loyal and faithful to God. I am reminded that everyone born of God conquers and overcomes the world, and my faith is the ultimate victory that overcomes all obstacles.

Scriptures: 1 John 5:4; 2 Chron. 16:9

Acceleration

Father, thank you for not withholding any good thing from me and for Your unwavering generosity. My life is in Your hands, and I eagerly look forward to Your perfect timing with great anticipation: that *Kairos* moment in my life when, at the appointed time, Your purpose is unfolded and manifested visibly in my life, and You act powerfully on my behalf.

When Isaac sowed and reaped a hundredfold harvest in the same year, You blessed him. He began to prosper and became rich. Isaac continued to prosper, and his wealth continued to grow, eventually making him extremely wealthy and prosperous. I ask You to do the same for me, Lord! Accelerate Your word to perform it and bring it to fruition.

Yes, indeed, it won't be long now—God's Decree. Things will happen so fast my head will swim, one blessing following another on its heels. I will not be able to keep up. Everything will be happening at once—and everywhere I look, blessings are coming from every direction! Blessings like wine pouring off the mountains and hills. You will make everything right again for me and restore everything to its proper state.

Father, I am deeply grateful that You are making me whole and have a beautiful future in store for me. The race is not given to the swift, but to those who endure to the end. Behold, You are doing a new thing and ushering in a new chapter in my life. You will even make a road in the wilderness and rivers in the desert. Thank you for prospering me and instilling a hope-filled future within me.

Scriptures: Gen. 26:12-13; Amos 9:11-13; Ps. 84:11; Ecc. 9:11; Is 43:19; Ps. 31:15; Jer. 29:11

Perpetual Victory

The Lord my God wins victory after victory and is always with me. God always causes me to triumph perpetually. No good thing will He withhold from me. I am more than a conqueror. The Lord goes with me, fights my battles against my enemies, and gives me victory. Therefore, I am not afraid. My spiritual army is not only greater but far more powerful than my enemies. Open my spiritual eyesight and allow me to see horses, fire chariots, and the angels encamped around me. God has given me victory over every adversary, and not a single enemy, not one, is able to stand or prevail against me. I am grateful for Your unwavering presence and protection. You are my Banner, my Victory, my Jehovah-Nissi.

Scriptures: Zep. 3:17; Rom. 8:36; Deut. 20:4; Jos. 10:8; 1 Cor. 15:57; 2 Kings 6:16-17; Exo. 17:15

Addressing Fear

Meditation

The entrance of Your world gives light and understanding to the simple. Therefore, I set my mind on the things of the Spirit. This book of the law shall not depart from my mouth, but I shall meditate and mutter on it day and night until it saturates my heart, spirit, soul, and mind. I am fully committed and will do everything written in it. Then You, God, will make my way prosperous, and then I will succeed. I am like a tree planted by the rivers of water that bring forth its fruit in its season because I am firmly and deeply rooted in You and unwavering in my discipline of meditation. My leaf also does not wither, and whatever I do it prospers. I will always bless the Lord, and His praise shall continually be in my mouth. I meditate on Your glorious work. I meditate on whatever is true, noble, just, pure, lovely, of good report, virtuous, and praiseworthy. I set my mind on things above, not on things on the earth. For You, Christ died for me, and my life is hidden in You.

Scriptures: Ps. 1:1-3; Phil. 4:4-9; Col. 3:1-3; Rom. 8:5-7; Heb. 3:1; Ps. 145:5

My Encompassing Shield

The Lord God is my Strength, my personal bravery, and my invincible army; He makes my feet like hinds' feet and will make me walk without being paralyzed by fear and terror. I will walk and make spiritual progress upon my high places of trouble, suffering, or responsibility with His help! The LORD is my impenetrable shield. My heart trusts Him with unwavering confidence, and I am helped. Therefore, my heart greatly rejoices. I shall thank Him and praise Him with my song. You are the horn of my salvation, my stronghold. You are my glory and the one who lifts up my head.

Scriptures: Hab. 2; Ps. 28:7; Ps. 18:3; Ps. 3:3

911 – Psalms 91

I dwell in the secret place of the Most-High, and I abide under the shadow of the Almighty. I will say of the Lord, "He is my refuge and my fortress; My God, in Him I will trust." Surely, He shall deliver me from the snare of the fowler and from the perilous pestilence. He shall cover me with His feathers, and under His wings, I shall take refuge; His truth shall be my shield and buckler. I shall not be afraid of the terror by night. Nor of the arrow that flies by day. Nor of the pestilence that walks in darkness. Nor of the destruction that lays waste at noonday.

A thousand may fall at my side, and ten thousand at my right hand, but it shall not come near me. Only with my eyes shall I look and see the reward of the wicked because I have made the Lord, who is my refuge, even the Most-High, my dwelling place. No evil shall befall me. Nor shall any plague come near my dwelling; For He shall give His angels charge over me, to keep me in all my ways. They shall bear me up in their hands, lest I dash my foot against a stone. I shall tread upon the lion and the cobra, the young lion and the serpent, I shall trample underfoot.

Because I have set my love upon God, therefore will He deliver me. He will set me on high because I have known His name. I shall call upon God, and He will answer me. He will be with me in trouble; He will deliver me and honor me. With long life shall He satisfy me and show me His salvation.

Scriptures: Ps. 91

I Am Victorious

Faith is acting on what I believe. It's a driving force. My actions and conduct align with what I believe God will do for me. Therefore, I have faith for more than ever before and step out in faith on the Word of God. Your word says it's impossible to please You, God, without faith. I desire to please You. I will not fear what God has told me to do. My faith is the victory that overcomes the world.

Faith is a spiritual law. In the kingdom, everything that exists is activated by the law of faith. Therefore, I choose to live by faith daily. I am determined to fight the good fight of faith. It's a constant battle, but I am confident that I will emerge victorious. I always win! Faith works by love. Faith is the victory that overcomes the world. Because I am born of God, I prevail, conquer, defeat, and overcome the world. I am victorious; this is the victory that conquers the world, even my faith, which is the ultimate conqueror.

Scriptures: Heb. 11:6; Ps. 118:6; 1 Tim. 6:12; 1 John 5:4; Gal. 5:6

The Faith Fight

No weapon that the enemy forms against me shall prosper. It won't succeed. Anyone who accuses me will be proven wrong, and their accusations will be shown to be false and erroneous. My legacy as a servant of the Lord includes peace, righteousness, security, triumph over the opposition, and proof that I am not guilty. Yes, vindication. I submit myself, therefore, to God. I resist the devil, and he will flee from me. The Lord causes my enemies who rise against me to be defeated and scattered before me.

They shall come out against me one way and flee before me seven ways. I give the devil no opportunity. For I do not wrestle against flesh and blood, but against the rulers, against the authorities, against the cosmic powers over this present darkness, against the spiritual forces of evil in the heavenly places. Blessed be the Lord, my rock, who trains my hands for war and my fingers for battle, causing me to be victorious. I fought the good fight of faith, and I won!

Scriptures: Is. 54:17; James 4:7; Ps. 68:1; Deut. 28:7; Eph. 6:12; Ps. 144:1; 1 Tim. 6:12

Seeking God's Protection

I will lift up my eyes to the hills— From whence comes my help. My help *comes* from the Lord, who made heaven and earth. He will not allow my foot to be moved; He who keeps me will not slumber. Behold, He who keeps Israel shall neither slumber nor sleep. The Lord is my keeper and my shade at my right hand. The sun shall not strike me by day, nor the moon by night. The Lord shall preserve me from all evil; He shall preserve my soul. The Lord shall preserve my going out and my coming in from this time forth and even forevermore.

Scriptures: Ps. 121:1-8

When I Am Afraid/Fearful And Need Protection

Even though I walk through the darkest valley, I will fear no evil, for You are with me; Your rod and Your staff comfort me. I sought the Lord, and He delivered me from all my fears. I will not fear those who can physically harm my body because more than 72,000 angels surround me, and God gives His angels charge over me.

God has not given me a spirit of fear but of power, love, and a sound mind. The Lord is my helper, and I will not fear what man can do to me. The Lord is on my side. I trust in the Lord, for He is my help, strength, song, and salvation. He preserves me from all evil and preserves my soul. The LORD guard me as I go out and as I come in. He guards me in everything that I do.

Scriptures: Ps. 23:4; Ps. 34:4; Matt. 10:28; Matt. 26: 53; 2 Tim. 1:7; Heb. 13:6; Is. 12:2; Ps. 121:7-8

A Kingdom That Can't Be Shaken/Unshakeable Kingdom

I live in and serve in a kingdom that is firm and stable. It cannot be shaken. It cannot be destroyed. Even when I hear of wars and rumors of wars, I will not be afraid. I will not be frightened when nations rise against nations and kingdom against kingdom. I will not be troubled when famines and earthquakes occur in different parts of the world. I am ready for Your coming. I am a wise man/woman who built my house on the rock. So, when the rain descends, and the floods come, and the winds blow and beat on my home, it will not fall because it is founded on the rock. My confidence is in You.

The solid foundation of Your Kingdom will withstand the shaking, shifting, and fiery trials. A warning comes before destruction. Therefore, I make all the necessary preparations to ensure that there's food and all other necessary provisions to keep us alive. Please keep my family and me safe within the ark. I unequivocally love and obey You, God. I pray that my family and I find grace in Your sight as I walk daily with You. Just like Noah pleased You, I please You, God. I have not been foolish by building my house on the sand. I stand on the solid rock of Your foundation and do Your sayings. You said, Lord, "If my people, who are called by Your name, will humble themselves, pray, seek Your face, and turn from their wicked ways, then I will hear from heaven, forgive their sin, and heal the Land." Heal the land, Lord, and protect my family.

Scriptures: Heb. 12:28-29; Matt. 24: 6-13; Matt. 7:24-27; Jer. 17:7; Gen. 7; Gen. 6:8; 2 Chron. 7:14

Casting My Care

Father, You bore me on eagles' wings and brought me to Yourself. As I wait upon You, Lord, renew my strength. I mount up with wings like eagles. I cast my cares on You, Lord, and You sustain me. You will never let the righteous be shaken. So, I cast all my anxieties on You because You care for me. I will not fear because You are with me. I will not be dismayed, for You are my God. You will strengthen and help me; You will uphold me with Your righteous right hand. Therefore, I am not anxious about anything, but in every situation, by prayer and petition, I present my requests to You with thanksgiving. And the peace of God, which transcends all understanding, guards my heart and mind in Christ Jesus. You give me rest from all my worries and burdens. I humble myself under God's mighty hand that He may lift me up in due time. I cast all my anxiety on Him because He cares for me. You have told me these things so I may have peace in You. In this world, I will have trouble. But I take heart because You have overcome the world.

Scriptures: Exo. 19:4; Is. 40:31; 1 Pet. 6-:7; Is. 41:10; Phil. 4:6-7; John 16:33

Facing Trials

I will trust in the Lord at all times. God is my refuge, and I pour out my heart to You. I consider it pure joy whenever I face trials of any kind. I know that the testing of my faith produces perseverance. Perseverance will perfect me so that I may be mature and complete, lacking nothing. I am not anxious about anything, but in every situation, by prayer and petition, I present my requests to God with thanksgiving.

I am joyful, hopeful, patient in affliction, and faithful in prayer. I maintain peace. I know that in this world, I will face tribulation. I take heart! I have overcome this world. I persevere under trial because, when I have stood the test, I will receive the crown of life that the Lord has promised to those who love Him. I trust in the LORD with all my heart and lean not on my own understanding. I do these three things to ensure my victory:

- Rejoice always,
- Pray continually and,
- Give thanks in all circumstances because this is God's will for me in Christ Jesus.

Scriptures: Ps. 62:8; Ps. 46; James 1:2-4; Rom. 12:12; Phil. 4:6; Is. 26:3-4; John 16:33; Prov. 3:5-6; 1 Thess. 5:16-18

Victory Over the Storm

One day, this burden will be taken away from my shoulder, and the yoke from my neck will be destroyed, all because of the anointing oil. I am overflowing with gratitude to God, who always leads me to triumphant victory in Christ. He leads me from place to place in one perpetual victory parade.

You tell me these things so that I may have perfect peace and unwavering confidence in You. I will undoubtedly face tribulation, trials, distress, and frustration in this world, but I must be of good cheer, take courage, be confident, certain, and undaunted! I refuse to be disheartened, for You have overcome the world. You have deprived it of the power to harm me and have conquered it for me. I maintain good spirits and take heart, for there will be no loss of life.

I am not frightened. I keep my courage high, for I have faith and complete confidence in God that it will be exactly as He said. I eat some food to fortify my strength, knowing that not a single hair from my head will perish. When I cried out to the Lord in my trouble, He brought me out of my distress. He stilled the storm to a whisper; the waves of the sea were hushed. He guided me to my desired haven. I will praise the LORD for his unfailing love and wonderful deeds for mankind.

Scriptures: Is: 10:27; 2 Cor. 2:14-16; 2 Cor. 1:7; Col. 2:6-9; John 16:33; Act 27: 22-38; Ps. 18:6; Ps. 107:29-31

Speak to the Storm

I choose to exercise my dominion mandate with confidence. When I confidently speak to the storm, "Peace! Be still," it must obey me. I put everything I have learned, received, or heard into practice, and the God of peace is with me. God leaves His peace with me. His peace is unlike anything that the world gives and surpasses it. I will not let my heart be troubled, and I will not be afraid.

I remain in perfect peace, and my mind is steadfast because I trust in God. I am not anxious about anything, but in every situation, I will make my requests to God through prayer and petition, with thanksgiving. And the peace of God, which transcends all understanding, guards my heart and my mind in Christ Jesus.

When I pass through the waters, I am confident that God is with me. When I pass through the rivers, they will not sweep over me. When I walk through the fire, I will not be burned. The flames will not consume me. I have great, unwavering faith, and I will not be afraid. I focus wholeheartedly on whatever is true, whatever is noble, whatever is right, whatever is pure, whatever is lovely, whatever is admirable — if anything is excellent or praiseworthy, I think about such things.

Scriptures: Mark 4:39; Phil. 4:7-9; Is; 26:3; Is. 43:2

Peace in the Storm

God, You are my refuge and my strength, a very present help in trouble. Grant me the serenity and confidence to sleep peacefully like You do whenever I face any kind of storm. Even though I may bend and sway like the palm tree in the storm, I remain unbroken. I will not break. I am righteous, and I flourish like the palm tree. Therefore, I will not fear. You calmed the storm, hushed it with a gentle whisper, and stilled the waves in my life.

I was glad because of the calm, especially when You guided me safely to my destination. I praise You, Lord, for Your loving kindness towards me and all of Your wonderful deeds! I follow Your lead even in the face of fear, worry, and anxiety. Even when I am terrified, petrified, worried, anxious, and scared, I will imitate You. You subdued the wind, and it ceased; You spoke to the waves, and they were still. I stand boldly, confidently, and unwavering in faith, speaking peace to my storm, knowing that You are my support. I can trust You for wisdom, guidance, and protection. Because You have my back, I remain in perfect peace, undaunted, and unwavering because I trust in You. I remain still, knowing that You are my God.

Scriptures: Is. 46:1; Matt. 8:23-27; Ps. 92: 12-13; Ps. 107: 29-31; Eph. 5:1; Mark 4:39; Ps. 46:10

Overcoming Fear

I sought the LORD, and He answered me; He delivered me from all my fears. I will not fear because He is with me; I will not be dismayed, for You are my God. Strengthen me and help me. Uphold me with Your righteous right hand. Because I dwell in the secret place of the Most High, I rest in the shadow of the Almighty. The LORD is my refuge and fortress, my God, whom I trust. Surely, You will save me from the fowler's snare and the deadly pestilence. He covers me with his feathers, and under his wings I find refuge; his faithfulness is my shield and armor. I will not fear the terror of night nor the arrow that flies by day.

The Lord is strong on my behalf. I lift up my eyes to the hills, knowing from where my help comes. My help comes from the LORD, who made heaven and earth. You will not allow my foot to slip. You will neither slumber briefly nor sleep soundly. You are my keeper. You are the shade on my right hand. The sun will not smite me by day, nor the moon by night. The LORD will protect me from all evil; You will keep my life. You will guard my going out and my coming in [everything that You do] from this time forth and forever.

Scriptures: Ps. 34:4; Is. 41:10; Ps. 91:1-6; 2 Chron. 16:9; Ps. 121:1-8

Shake it off

God guarantees my safe passage in life. His Word stands forever. I cling tightly and hold on firmly to the Word of God and His amazing promises. I choose to remain rooted and grounded in Him. Disappointments, discouragement, pain, heartache, trials, and storms may come, but these are temporary situations. I keep my eyes fixed solely upon Him and do not become distracted or swayed by the storms of life. I listen intently to Jesus' voice in the midst of the chaos and storms. He is my guide and protector. I will arise and shake off this adversity, suffering no ill effects. It will be as if nothing touched me, and I will emerge unharmed and emboldened in my faith. I declare that nothing can harm me. I stand invincible, and I shake off every setback. I receive my victory right now! My day of deliverance is here!!!!

Scriptures: Prov. 4:25; Acts 28:5; Mark 12:18; 2 Cor. 6:2; Eph. 3:14; Heb 12:2
Overcoming the Fear of Death

Life and death are shaped by the words I speak. I commit to choosing my words and thoughts carefully. I declare faith-filled affirmations over my life, believing that God will grant me a long and fulfilling life. Your word dwells richly in me, and I fill my heart with Your Word. I guard my heart, for it is the wellspring of life. I actively embrace faith and courage in the face of my challenges. I refuse to be immobilized by fear or succumb to a premature death. I shall live fully and proclaim the greatness of the LORD. I renounce the spirit of fear regarding an early demise.

No one or nothing can harm me. I fear no evil, for You are at my side; I triumph over every form of adversity. I proclaim God's supernatural protection, power, and provision over my life. I will fulfill my purpose and destiny, achieving remarkable feats and performing strong exploits because I collaborate with the Almighty. I remain resilient and steadfast. Your plans for me are good, intended for my welfare, promising me a hopeful future.

I am spiritually empowered. I uphold Your Word, fully aware that I will see no death. Jesus conquered death and disarmed the devil, liberating me from the grasp of the fear of dying. I will forge a new path forward in my mind, thoughts, and attitudes. And when my appointed time arrives, as determined by the Lord, I will be truly blessed, resting from my labor, knowing my good deeds, good name, and legacy will endure. I thank You for finishing grace.

Scriptures: Prov. 18:12; Ps. 118:17; John 8:51; Ps. 23:4; Rev. 14:13; Col. 3:16; Prov. 4:23; Jer. 29:11

A Resilient Spirit

Joy Is My Weapon

Joy is my bold proclamation of faith. When I abide in Your love and adhere to Your commandments, it's the source of my strength, demonstrating the Spirit and God's power within me. It's an impenetrable shield of defense against the enemy's fiery darts. I refuse to cower and tremble in the enemy's presence because I am as bold as a lion. I embrace and exercise my dominion mandate with unwavering courage, strength, valor, and dignity. I know who I am and whose I am. I walk and talk like God, exercising my rights of nobility and royalty as a Kingdom citizen. I wield the sword of the spirit, praying in my heavenly language and engaging in praise and worship. God's super on my natural is my offensive weapon.

Joy is a powerful and transformative force that strengthens and empowers me spiritually till my heart overflows. I rejoice aloud and sing joyfully because the Holy One of Israel is with me. Your steadfast love gives me great joy, and I am crowned with everlasting joy. As a member of the Kingdom of God, I am blessed to experience joy, a vital fruit of the Spirit, which is instrumental in my spiritual growth.

I walk daily with God. Therefore, gladness and joy will pursue and overtake me while sorrow and sighing flee away. A joyful heart is a powerful medicine, but a crushed spirit dries up the bones and leads to depression and despair. Even in the midst of my trials and tribulations, I choose to rejoice because I have the revelation that joy always comes in the morning. I find fullness of joy in Your presence and pleasures forevermore at Your right hand.

Scriptures: Neh. 8:10; John 15:10-11; Ps. 90:14; Is. 51:11; Rom. 14:17; Gal. 5:22; Gen. 5:22; Prov. 17:22; Ps. 16:11; Ps. 30:5; Acts. 5:41

The Strong Spirit of a Man

Strength and vitality come from abiding in You. My consistent and daily walk with You strengthens my inner man. I meditate on scripture, read my Word, and journal to hear what You say. This spiritual regime prepares me and increases my confidence. I am assured that the Lord will strengthen and help me fight my battles. When trials and tribulations come, I will rejoice in hope, be patient in tribulation, and remain continually persistent in prayer.

My spirit will not be broken, because it is strong and healthy. God has not given me a spirit of fear but of power, love, and a sound mind. The word says a strong spirit of a man sustains him in bodily pain or trouble. I will be blessed when I remain steadfast under trial, for when I have stood the test, I will receive the crown of life, which God promised me because I love him. I can do everything through Christ, who gives me strength. I am more than an overcomer!

Scriptures: John 15:4-5; Josh. 1:8; Ps. 18:32-39; Rom. 12:12; Prov. 18:14; 2 Tim. 1:7; Prov. 18:14-16; James 1:12; Phil. 4:13; Rom. 8:37

Strength

Father, when my flesh and my heart fail me, strengthen my heart because You are my portion forever. I come to You because I am weary and burdened, so You can give me rest. Your power is greatest in my weakness. Because You are within me, I will not fail. It is You who arms me with strength and makes my way perfect. You give power to the weak and strength to the powerless. You make my feet like the feet of deer and set me on my high places. I will lift up my eyes to the mountains, knowing from where my help comes. My help comes from the Lord, the Maker of heaven and earth.

Scriptures: Ps. 59:16; Is. 40:29; Ps. 73:26; Exo 15: 2-3; Ps. 121:2-3; Ps. 73:26; Ps. 68:35; 2 Cor. 12:9; Neh. 8:10; Ps. 46:5

Pillar of Strength

The Lord is my strength and my shield; my heart trusts in Him, and He helps me. The Lord is my strength and my song. He has given me victory. This is my God, and I praise him and exalt him. My heart leaps for joy when I praise him with song. I remain vigilant, standing firm in the faith, courageous, and strong. The joy of the Lord is my strength.

Therefore, I can do all things through Christ who strengthens me. You, God, are awesome; You are the God of Israel who gives power and strength to Your people. I am blessed when I remain steadfast under trial, for when I have stood the test, I will receive the crown of life, which God has promised to those who love Him. So, I sing of Your strength; in the morning, I sing of Your love, for You are my fortress, my refuge in times of trouble. You are my pillar of strength.

Scriptures: Ps. 28:7; 1 Cor. 16:13; Exo. 15:2; Phil. 4:13; James 1:12-14

The Joy of the Lord is My Strength

When I dwell and abide in Your presence through consistent prayer, heartfelt praise, worship, and studying Your word, the joy of the Lord becomes my strength. I will not be shaken when trials and tribulations arise because I am rooted in You. You are the shield that surrounds me. Therefore, my joy can be complete, and I can bear much fruit. I remain closely and vitally united with You, making my home in You, and Your words reside within my heart so I can ask for whatever I want and desire, and I can be completely confident that You will grant my request.

Scriptures: Neh. 8:10; John 15

The Crown of Life/The Victor's Crown

I joyfully and eagerly desire to serve You, Lord, not motivated by the benefits You will give me, but out of a pure heart of love filled with gratitude and passion for all You have done for me. You entrusted everything to my care, and I will perform those responsibilities with a spirit of excellence that is pleasing to You. I maintain a good example to bring never-ending glory, honor, and praise to You, my Great Shepherd.

I endure temptation, testing, and suffering with courage. I will not fear it but endure with faithfulness unto death, knowing that I will be blessed and approved and one day receive the crown of life, the victor's crown, that You, Lord, have faithfully promised to those who love You.

Scriptures: 2 Tim. 2:3; James 1:12; Ps. 25

Firmly Rooted

I do not fear because the Lord is with me. I am not dismayed because God strengthens and helps me. He upholds me with His righteous right hand. I keep my eyes always on the Lord. With Him at my right hand, I will not be shaken. I am blessed because I trust and have confidence in the Lord. I am like a tree planted by the water, sending out its roots by the stream. It does not fear the heat; its leaves are always green. It has no worries in a year of drought and never fails to bear fruit. I am the righteous, and I cannot be uprooted.

Scriptures: Is. 41:10; Ps. 16:8; Jer. 17:7-8; Ps. 112:7; Prov. 10:30

Remaining Strong In A Crisis

Father, You said in Your Word, "If I fall to pieces in a crisis, it reveals that my foundation is weak and there wasn't much to me in the first place." I ask You to empower and equip me so that I won't fall apart in a crisis. By meditating on Your Word, I gain confidence in the strength You have instilled in me, knowing there's so much more to me than a temporary moment of weakness and breakdown. Jesus, You remained on the cross and refused to cave in or give up despite all that You encountered. Therefore, I commit to standing firm and resolute when trouble comes. I am not weak, fainthearted, or cowardly.

I am mentally strong. I am resilient. I possess fortitude. I am mentally tough and not weak. I seek courage and perseverance, so I will not faint or give up. I draw confidently near the throne of grace to receive mercy and help in the time of need, knowing that Your grace is all I need, for Your power is the greatest when I am weak.

When my flesh and heart fail, You, God, are my strength and portion forever. Although my soul is weary with sorrow, strengthen me according to Your word, and I will remain firm in faith. You give strength to Your people, increase the power of the weak, and bless Your people with peace. My flesh and heart may fail, but it is in You, God, that I find my heart's strength and portion forever.

Scriptures: Prov. 24:10; 2 Cor. 12:9; Ps. 73:26; 1 Cor. 16:13; Is. 40:29; Ps. 119:28; Ps. 29:11; Ps. 73:26

Finishing Strong: A Confession for Caregivers

Fear not, loved one. Don't be afraid! I'd like to show God's kindness to you and do something special for you, as a result of a vow I made. I will restore to you all that belonged to you previously, and you shall live here with me and eat meals at my table. Whether I am honoring my parents out of love and obedience to God or taking care of someone else in need, I receive the promise that all may go well with me and I will live long and enjoy life. I will not look after my own interests but the interests of others. Do not urge me to leave you or to return from following you. For where you go, I will go, and where you lodge, I will lodge. Your people shall be my people, and your God my God. Where you die, I will die, and there will I be buried. May the LORD do so to me and more also if anything but death parts me from you.

Lord, I have undertaken a challenging task, one that demands immense patience. As their bodies weaken and their health continues to decline, I ask You to strengthen and prepare me so I can be more diligent and patient in my caregiving. Grant me patience and compassion so I don't become frustrated with them when they forget or make mistakes. I vow not to bring up painful memories or discuss topics that may upset them. With Your guidance, I can navigate the challenges of caregiving with grace and understanding.

At times, the weight of this responsibility feels overwhelming. There are moments when I feel isolated and resentful. In these times, I have come to realize the importance of support. Lord, I ask You to send others to assist me and grant me a time of rest, relief, and recuperation. I seek rest that can only come from You. I am ready to take Your yoke, learn from You, and embrace gentleness and humility. I will encourage myself in You, affirming my capacity to persevere, keep going, see the bright side, and maintain resilience, because a cheerful heart and laughter are indeed good medicine.

Moreover, You came with Your love and kept me steady when I felt my feet slipping. Comfort me and make me feel secure when I am burdened with worries. You know everything about me, including my desire to remain faithful in love and service, as well as the perseverance I have demonstrated. I will run the race that is set before me with endurance and finish strong. Help me also to guide them to finish their race with dignity, honor, strength, and grace.

Scriptures: 2 Sam. 9:3-7; Heb. 4:16; Exo. 20:12; Eph. 6:2-3; Ruth 1:16-17; Ps. 94:18-19; Phil. 2:3-4; Matt. 11:28-30; Rev. 2:19

Sweet Sleep

Sweet Sleep

Lord, You refresh my soul. You make me lie down in green pastures. You encourage me to come to You when I am weary and burdened, and You will give me rest. I am Your beloved, and You give me sweet sleep. I will lie down in peace and sleep. For You alone, O Lord, make me dwell in safety. You neither slumber nor sleep. You watch over me and will not let my foot slip. Because I dwell in the shelter of the Most-High, I will rest in the shadow of the Almighty because You are my refuge and my fortress, my God, in whom I trust. When You cradle me in Your bosom, deep sleep will fall upon me, my sleep will be sweet while You sustain me, and I will not be afraid.

Scriptures: Ps. 23:2-3; Matt. 11:28-30; Prov. 3:24; Ps. 4:8; Ps. 127:2; Ps. 121:1-4; Ps. 91:1-2; Is. 46:4

Rest For The Weary

Father, I come to You because I am weary and burdened. You promised to give me rest. I take Your yoke upon me and learn from You, for You are gentle and humble in heart, and I will find rest for my soul. Your yoke is easy, and Your burden is light. I am Your beloved, and You cradle me in Your bosom, and because I work hard, I sleep well. In a dream, in a vision of the night, when deep sleep falls on me as I sleep in my bed, I lay down and slept, and I awoke, for the Lord sustained me. When my mind stays on You, You keep me in perfect peace.

Scriptures: Matt. 11:28-30; Job 33:15; Ps. 3:5; Is. 26:3

Waiting On God

God, unfold Your plan and purpose for my life. Your timing is perfect. I wait for You, Lord. I expectantly wait, and in Your Word do, I hope. Waiting on You, Lord, is not easy; It is immensely challenging. I ask You to give me a promise to hold onto because it helps me manage my expectations and keeps the vision before me. I seek direction and wisdom while waiting, so I do not stray from the will of God. I know there's a purpose for waiting.

I wait for clear direction as You build my character, resilience, humility, and compassion. You see the beginning from the end. So, I will not rush ahead of You, linger behind You, or step out of Your will. I will wait with a great attitude. I will not complain, grumble, or become frustrated with having my own immediate needs, impulses, or desires satisfied. I will not test You, nag You, or forget Your works. Do not grant me my request and then send emptiness into my soul or afflict me with disease or death. Your grace is sufficient for me. Your power is made perfect in my weakness. Your power rests upon me. For when I am weak, then I am strong.

I walk step in step with You with a great attitude. I wait patiently, quietly, and expectantly because I know I will not lose the promise that rightfully belongs to me. My heart takes courage while I wait for the Lord! The Lord is good to those waiting for Him and the soul seeking Him. You shall strengthen my heart, and I will see the goodness of the Lord in the land of the living.

Scriptures: Lam. 3:15; Ps. 130; Ps. 27; 2 Cor. 12:8-10

Victory in Court Cases

You are my shield and exceedingly great reward. And when they bring me to trial and deliver me to the judge, I will not be anxious beforehand about what I am to say. I will say whatever is given to me by the Holy Spirit in that hour because He speaks and not me. Who can be successful against me if God is for me and on my side? I will not have an anxious heart. I will be strong and fear not!

Behold, my God comes with vengeance, with the recompense of God. You will come and save me and not let my foot slip. No weapon formed against me shall prosper. The Lord will cause the enemies who rise up against me to be defeated. They will come out against me one way but flee before me seven ways. The Lord will conquer my enemies when they attack me. They will attack me from one direction but scatter from me in seven.

Scriptures: Gen. 15:1; Luke 12:11-12; Rom. 8:21; Deut. 28:7; Ps. 35:1; Eph. 6:16

The Nation

Healing the Nations

If my people who are called by my name will humble themselves and pray and seek my face and turn from their wicked ways, then I will hear from heaven and will forgive their sin and heal their land. We bless Israel because You said, "Bless Israel." We lift up Your chosen people, Israel, as You have commanded us against all the threats against them, Hezbollah, Iraq, and all other enemies. Send help to Israel, strength, and a breakthrough. Rescue them from every evil attack, for You are a strong fortified tower. The righteous run into it and are safe. In peace, they will lie down and sleep, for You alone, LORD, make them dwell in safety. Thank you for being their refuge and strength, an ever-present help in their time of trouble. Though they walk in the midst of trouble, You preserve their lives. You stretch out Your hand against their enemies, and with Your right hand, You save them.

I pray for Gaza and command peace to reign in the region. We call for a ceasefire among all global conflicts, wars, civil wars, skirmishes, and coups d'état. I lift the war between Russia and Ukraine. Help Ukraine not to be fainthearted, afraid, terrified, or give way to panic. Go before them and fight against their enemies to give them victory. LORD, You are the Rock, who trains Your people's hands for war and fingers for battle. You are a loving God and fortress, their stronghold and deliverer, their shield, in whom they take refuge, who subdues peoples under Yourself. O LORD, what is man that You care for him, the son of man that You think of him?

I pray for the Pro-Palestinian conflict and command it to cease in the name of Jesus. Open their eyes to the truth, Lord, about whom to support. We pray for food insecurity and famine across all the nations: Gaza, Mali, Sudan, Afghanistan, Congo, El Salvador, Ethiopia, and Haiti. I pray for the safety of humanitarian workers, that they will maintain their courage and boldness, and move forward to serve those who are most in need. Help the humanitarian workers to do the will of the Father. You said, "If we give food to all flesh, Your mercy will endure forever." You are the Bread of Life, and we come to You so we can never hunger and thirst.

Strengthen the people's hearts, Lord. You are the God who sees and hears and makes provision. Father, I know You respond to the cries of the children. Help them to arise, hold their hand, and have hope and courage in their soul, knowing that You will bring provision. Let their children live and not die. Provide wells in the desert and be with the children.

I pray that every human trafficker is captured and arrested by the Holy Spirit. Pour out Your spirit on all flesh. Let conviction arise and overwhelm them in their spirit. Turn the brothels into trade and vocational schools that glorify You. I pray for laborers who rescue trafficked women and help them heal in their souls. Let them experience Your touch, which brings wholeness from traumatic experiences and speaks prosperity to their souls.

We bind the spirit of depression and anxiety. Lord our God, we call out to You for help to heal them. You, Lord, bring them up from the realm of the dead and spare them from going down to the pit of depression. For You are our Shepherd and therefore we lack nothing. Make them lie down in green pastures, and lead them beside the still quiet waters, and refresh their soul. And when they walk through the darkest valley, help them to fear no evil. Remind them that You are with them and that Your rod and Your staff comforts them. Help them to fear not, for You have redeemed them. You have called them by Your name.

They belong to You. When they pass through the waters, You will be with them; when they go through the rivers, it shall not overflow them. When they walk through the fire, they shall not be burned, nor shall the flame scorch them. Help them to trust You because You are a faithful God whose Word never returns void to You. Therefore, rescue them, and help them to flee in safety because they trust in You, so they will not be disappointed. Raise up godly leaders who will lead reforms on crime, immorality, wars, violence, lawlessness, and all manner of evil. Let prevention be at the top of Your mind. Let protection be at the top of Your mind. Let prosecution be at the top of Your mind, partnerships, and policy. We bind crime, immorality, wars, violence, and all manner of evil.

I exercise dominion and power on the earth given to me by God. God is strong, and He wants me to be strong. According to John 14:12, I will do even greater works than Jesus. Prayer, praise, worship, and decrees are my spiritual weapons. They are well-made weapons that create an atmosphere conducive for God to dwell in. No hand-to-hand combat is necessary because my presence shifts the atmosphere. I am the thermostat that brings love, joy, peace, unity, godliness, and decency into every situation. Lust, envy, strife, carnality, and all manner of wickedness can't exist or operate around me. I am called to be the salt and the light in dark places.

Scriptures: John 14:12; Matt. 5:13-16; Eph. 6:12

Praying For Our Educational Institutions And Schools

God, You promise to give people a future and a hope. Set Your Angels around all school systems and colleges to guard and defend every day. Keep our schools and colleges safe from danger with a divine circle of protection with the angel of the Lord. Uncover and reveal any plots of harm and violence before they take shape and are executed. The fear of the LORD is the beginning of knowledge.

The Bible is a valuable guide for teaching, correcting, and training in righteousness. Equip all college and school personnel – presidents, superintendents, principals, teachers, teacher's aids, professors, school counselors, food service workers, students, custodians, school nurses, substitute teachers, athletic directors, and all other school and college personnel with perseverance, character, and hope to reintroduce Your presence and the Ten Commandments into our educational school systems and institutions.

From preschool to high school and college, encourage teachers to guide students in righteous living and instill values of character, hope, perseverance, and love for You. Let these teachings resonate deeply, ensuring that they remember the foundation laid from their youth, even in adulthood. Ignite within every student a burning passion for learning, empowering them to be well-informed and grasp new concepts quickly and enthusiastically.

Help them to be as zealous for You as they are for music, social media, TikTok, drugs, cellphones, and all other distractions. Remind them to focus on eternal things above, rather than on earthly, fleeting things. Help them understand and recognize that they can do all things through Christ, who strengthens them. By walking obediently in Your ways and following Your commands, the students will prosper in all their endeavors and wherever they go. Strengthen their resolve to remain steadfast in doing good, assuring them that they will reap the rewards in due season if they do not faint and give up.

Scriptures: Dan. 1:4; Acts 22:3; Prov. 22:6; 1 Cor. 10:31; 1 Kings 2:3; Prov. 1:7; Jer. 29:11; 2 Tim. 3:16-17; Phil. 4:13; Col. 3:2; Ps. 101:3; Ps. 34:7; Heb. 6:19; Ps. 34:7; Dan. 1:4; Rom. 5:4

The Incarcerated And Imprisoned

Father, I remember those in prison as if I, myself, were there. I can only imagine the heavy burden of guilt, the deep pain, the disappointment, and the overwhelming fear that envelops them. The anxiety, depression, and the crushing sense of hopelessness and isolation must weigh heavily, compounded by the mistreatment and abuse they encounter daily.

Father, send me, along with other ministers and Pastors, with a heart for the imprisoned. Let us be Your hands and feet, bringing good news to the oppressed, binding up the brokenhearted, proclaiming liberty to the captives, and releasing those held in chains and bondage. Because wherever the Spirit of the Lord is, there is freedom, and there is liberty.

Uproot the bitterness, the anger, the resentment, especially among those wrongly and unjustly imprisoned and mistreated. Help us demonstrate Your steadfast love so that one day, they, too, will proclaim the good news of God. Even on their deathbed, they will proclaim and accept Jesus as their personal Lord and Savior. It is Your will that not one of them shall perish or be lost forever. Help us to be bold and fearless in our evangelism.

I decree and declare a "suddenly," a sudden shift in their circumstances—a powerful earthquake of liberation that will break the shackles off their hearts and minds. Grant them divine favor with the judges and prosecutors, canceling sentences and recognizing time served for good behavior.

Nothing is impossible with You, God, and we thank you for the miraculous turnaround. Restore their hope and become a firm and secure anchor for their soul. Help us foster and cultivate an environment where faith and knowledge of You flourish, guiding future prisoners toward brighter days filled with healing and restoration.

Scriptures: Heb. 13:3; Is. 61:1; 2 Cor. 3:17; Luke 4: 17-21; Acts 5:17-32; Acts 12:1-18; Acts 16:16-40; Matt. 18:1-20; Matt. 25: 31-46

A Fire Fighter's Confession

Firefighters embody strength and courage, facing daunting challenges with unwavering resolve and without fear or terror. Remind them that the Lord goes before them, paving the way, and walks alongside them, never leaving or forsaking them. Even when they walk through the darkest valley of smoke, they need fear no evil, because You are their constant companion, providing them with comfort. The Lord prioritizes their protection and safety. God commands his angels to guard these men and women in all their endeavors. The Lord shields them from all harm—He watches over their lives and their coming and going both now and forevermore.

As the buildings, floors, and walls collapse around them, grant them agility and speed, like a deer's feet that can run and navigate swiftly and securely without stumbling or falling. Please give them a hearing ear and a seeing eye and equip them with the strength of Samson to rescue the fallen, the trapped, and the unconscious. Help the firefighters maneuver and navigate through perilous situations and circumstances so that they may live and not die. Illuminate their path, provide clear exits, and make a way of escape in the darkest moments.

I thank you for their dedicated service and for emulating and reflecting the Son of Man who did not come to be served but to serve and gave his life as a ransom for many. As they bravely run into danger, remind them that two are better than one, so together, they can lift those who need help. Their ongoing love, selfless acts, and good deeds are invaluable. They persevere under literal fiery trials, and because they have stood the test and stand firm and strong, they will one day receive the crown of life promised by the Lord.

Scriptures: Mark 10:45; Ecc. 4:9-10; Heb. 10:24; James 1:12; Prov. 20:12; 1 Cor. 10:13

A Police Officer's Confession

We thank you for our Police Officers, these brave men and women who willingly lay down their lives for others daily. We thank you for the police officers' boldness, courage, and willingness to take action, with an attitude of "Yes, here I am, send me," while others run and cower in fear and fright. This bravery demonstrates excellent love. Thanks for training their hands for war and their fingers for battle. You are their fortress, stronghold, deliverer, shield, in whom they take refuge. Because of Your steadfast love, You place a hedge of protection around them.

Help them to be strong in the Lord and the power of Your might. Remind them to put on their spiritual armor, the whole armor of God, that they may be able to stand against the devil's wiles. Lord, Your eyes are everywhere, in every place, beholding the evil and the good. Order their steps spiritually and naturally, and don't allow any iniquity to have dominion over them. Illuminate their path. May they learn and continue to do right, maintaining a good name. Place them among like-minded officers who uphold the standard of the law and avoid corruption and scandals.

As iron sharpens iron, so one police officer sharpens another. Remind them to slander no one, to be peaceable and considerate, and always to be gentle toward everyone. The use of excessive force, sexual harassment or assault, racial profiling, perjury, filing false police reports, unconstitutional searches and arrests, and planting, mishandling, or tampering with evidence shall not be named among them. Help them to hold fast to what is good, abstain from evil, and guard their heart, for everything they do flows from it.

Please help them to think critically on their feet by testing the spirits. They should not believe everything they hear. Please help them to be quick to listen and slow to speak.

Grant them excellent communication skills. Fill them with kindness, compassion, and forgiveness to foster strong relationships with those they serve. Help them cultivate a spirit of humility instead of a desire for power so they maintain a proper perspective and will not think of themselves more highly than they should.

Provide them generously with wisdom and discernment to avoid any traps and dangers that may come their way, including the agent of death. Help them defend the weak and the fatherless, uphold the cause of the poor and the oppressed, and rescue the weak and the needy while delivering them from the hands of the wicked. Establish the work of their hands.

We are grateful for their service; justice brings joy to the righteous community, but terror to those who do evil. Remind them that whatever they do, they should work at it wholeheartedly, as if serving the Lord. Help them not become weary in doing good, for in due time, God will richly reward them.

Scriptures: Gal. 6:9-10; Prov. 21:15; Ps. 90:17; James 1:5; Ps. 82:3-4; Rom. 12:3; Eph. 4:32; Tit. 3:1-2; Prov. 4:23; 1 Thess. 5:21; Is. 1:17; Ps. 119:105; Prov. 15:3; John 15:13; Ps. 144:1-2; Eph. 6:10-11; James 1:9

A Military Soldier's Confession

O God, hear my plea. Protect and preserve my life from my enemies. Shield me from their secret plots. Their weapons, including firearms, pistols, revolvers, machine guns, shotguns, assault rifles, grenade launchers, knives, bayonets, cannons, mortars, bombs, and rockets, are accurate and equipped with the latest military technology and innovation. Shield me and my platoon from the accuracy of these weapons. Disrupt the airwaves and let their weapons and missiles fail. They seek to ambush me and my platoon, attacking suddenly and fearlessly, killing us all. They continually seek evil against me, my comrades, and my country.

Defend me, God. Defend my fellow comrades and soldiers. Let the enemy's military schemes and plots fail and crumble before us. I can already foresee my miracle and deliverance right now because You are my refuge. Preserve my life from the enemy as I yearn to return home to my beloved spouse and children. When I am afraid, I put my trust in You. What can mere mortals do to me?

No weapon formed against me shall prosper. I will hold on; I will not falter, quit, or surrender because You are with me, empowering me to be more than a conqueror. Today, I put on the full armor of God and prepared to resist the forces of evil. I resolve to stand firm in the face of adversity. I fight for America, my country, my comrades, and my family. I will battle fiercely and triumph over the enemy.

God, You grant strength to the weak and power to the weary. Renew my strength and the strength of my platoon. Help us soar on wings like eagles, running without growing weary and walking without stumbling.

You commanded us to be strong and courageous! I will not tremble or be dismayed, for the Lord my God is with me wherever I go. I will take courage and heart because You have overcome the world.

I rejoice greatly in celebrating Your protection and deliverance. Restore, support, and strengthen me. Place me on a firm foundation. The Lord strengthens His people; bless me with peace and salvation! Together, we will arise and overcome.

Scriptures: Ps. 64; 1 Pet. 5:10; Jos. 1:9; Matt. 11:28-30; Is. 40:29-31; Eph. 6:13; John 16:33; Ps. 29:11; Ps. 116:6; Ps. 56:3-4

A Healthcare Worker's Confession

As a healthcare worker, I am like a lighthouse that helps people navigate, achieve dominion, and overcome the storms of sickness and disease. Grant me wisdom, knowledge, and understanding when conducting intakes, performing assessments, and diagnostic tests. Let me feel the reassurance of Your divine support, which I believe can prevent medical errors, such as delayed and inaccurate diagnoses or failures to communicate clearly with my patients. When challenged by insufficient staffing and resources, remind me that You are my source. I can walk forward with spiritual confidence and progress spiritually in my places of trouble, challenges, suffering, and responsibility. Please remind me to wear my personal protective equipment consistently and correctly to maintain and sustain my own health.

God, please help me keep a cool head when the patient and family escalate and become verbally and physically abusive toward me. Let my reasonableness be known to everyone. Empower me to remain vigilant for the patient or family member, ready to sound the alarm if I feel threatened or in danger. Fill me with compassion and empathy, increase my capacity to listen attentively, and open my heart to understanding. Please give me the ability to communicate clearly and simply. I believe this is key to reducing misunderstandings, building trust with my patients and their family members, which in turn leads to healthier outcomes.

I understand the value and importance of putting my own oxygen mask on first. Please remind me to do so often to manage the stress of my work. Self-care is a gift to myself, a testament to my value and the care I deserve. It also equips me to extend Your care to others. Please restore me spiritually, physically, and mentally from the strain of working more than 12 hours daily, including on-call hours and overtime. Renew my strength. Help me manage my workload to avoid burnout. Keep me fueled, energized, and resilient so that I don't give up during tough times. I commit to pray more fervently and frequently, casting all my cares and burdens upon You. I trust in Your divine support to help me manage my workload and prevent burnout.

All sufficiency is in You. Empower me to do all things in Christ so that through endurance and encouragement, I might have hope. Make me strong in Your spirit, and I can stand firm and handle every challenging situation I encounter. I am a healthcare hero serving as a beacon of hope and an angel to everyone I encounter in my daily work.

Scriptures: Col. 3:22-24; Mal. 4:2; Phil. 4:13; Rom. 15:4:2; 2 Cor. 3:5; Ps. 23:3; Is. 40:31; Rom. 12:11-13; Prov. 2:2; Phil. 4:5; Hab. 3:19

The Political System

Blessed is the nation whose God is the Lord. Our hope is in You. You bring to no effect the intention, thoughts, ideas, and purposes of Your creation that vigorously oppose, resist, and fight against Your divine plans and fail to promote and honor Your glory. The heart of the King is like channels of water in Your hands, and You turn it whichever way You wish. You commanded us to occupy, to be diligent and faithful in our responsibilities until You return.

Regardless of our political affiliations, we are called to respect and obey the rulers who have been placed in authority by God. We pray for them, knowing that God's hand guides their decisions. We intercede on their behalf, give thanks for them, and ask for God's help in their leadership. Our prayers for the President, Senators, House of Representatives, Congress, and all other government officials are a reflection of our desire to live peaceful and quiet lives marked by godliness and dignity. This action is good and pleases God.

People who oppose the authorities oppose what God has done. Presidents and leaders are a threat to evil people, not to good people. There is no need to be afraid. Just do right. We will not fear bad news.

We trust in the wisdom of the Lord to protect us from the deceitful and the wicked. Some may put their trust in earthly powers, but we place our trust in the name of the LORD our God, our refuge. We do not put our trust in mere mortals, for our confidence is in God alone. The Lord will deliver us from every evil attack. Our focus is on God, and He will keep us in perfect peace because our minds are steadfast on Him, the eternal rock.

Scriptures: Rev. 3:13; Prov. 21:1; Ps. 20:7; Ps. 118:8; Is. 26:3-4; 2 Tim. 4:18. Ps. 112:7; Prov. 2:12; 1 Tim. 2:1-3

A Fight to the Finish

And that about wraps it up. God is strong, and He wants you strong. So, take everything the Master has set out for you: well-made weapons of the best materials, and put them to use so you will be able to stand up to everything the devil throws your way. This is no weekend war that we'll walk away from and forget about in a couple of hours. This is for keeps, a life-or-death fight to the finish against the devil and all his angels.

Scriptures: Eph. 6:10-12

Bonus Confession

I remember the LORD my God: for it is He that giveth me power to get wealth that He may establish His covenant. And the LORD is with me, and I am prosperous in the house of my Pastor and at my place of employment. Moreover, my bosses, Pastor, and other church leaders trust me and are not concerned about my faithfulness and trustworthiness. And I am an attractive person and well-favored.

No power on earth can make a person important, wealthy, powerful, or significant. Promotion comes neither from the East nor from the West nor from the South. But God is the judge. He decides who will be important and necessary. He lifts one person up and brings another down.

I am obedient to my spouse, pastors, church leaders, and bosses; I am an example to believers in word, conduct, love, spirit, faith, and purity. I have purposed in my heart that I would not defile myself. My countenance glows with life and vitality. God, You are no respecter of persons, and Your Word says, "You will respond to anyone who will walk in obedient faith." I believe that all things are possible to the individual who believes.

I have an excellent spirit, an excellent spirit of integrity, knowledge, understanding, and the ability to interpret dreams, solve riddles, and explain enigmas. I operate in the word of wisdom, the word of knowledge, faith, the gifts of healing, the working of miracles, prophecy, discerning of spirits, divers kinds of tongues, and the interpretation of tongues. I am humble and possess a good, great, and excellent reputation which precedes me. I am ten times better than any individual I encounter. I am intelligent and have a clear understanding of all visions and dreams.

I give God credit for all the success in my life and for the ability to interpret dreams. The Lord is with me, and I am successful. My employers note that the Lord is with me and that the Lord makes everything that I do prosper. I find favor in my leaders' sight and serve them. My leaders trust me and give me great authority. The Lord is with me, and whatever I do, the Lord makes it prosper.

I remain true to my convictions. There is an individual on the earth in whom is the Spirit of the Holy God, and my name is _____. I pray daily on my knees, giving thanks to God. Because I believe in God by faith, I serve with justice and receive what God has promised me.

I am greatly beloved and very humble, more than all people who are on the face of the earth. I am accountable to God, and the fulfillment of my dream is entirely dependent upon God. Because God hath allowed all this, and there is none so discreet and wise as I, my Pastors trust me to be a leader. I serve others wholeheartedly and remain totally dependent on God. God will use me and my spouse to save His people and their families.

There is something different and unique about me. I have an excellent spirit. I exemplify Jesus. I have an excellent work ethic. I have an over-and-above work ethic and a great attitude. I give and then some. I do more than is required. I am going above and beyond my job description. Moreover, I do it with a smile. I say something encouraging to everyone each day. My value grows each day. I do everything wholeheartedly for the Lord, not for men, knowing that the Lord will provide the reward for my inheritance because I serve the Lord Jesus Christ.

There are hidden treasures in my place of employment. Therefore, I have a purpose for being at (_____). I choose to trust God and stay where I am. I have a good, great, and excellent reputation, and my colleagues hold me in high esteem. I am an employee who exercises influence. I am planted here to make an impact in Jesus' name. My work is a place of worship and service. I arise and shine. I stand up and stand out. God uses me where I am to glorify His name. Holy Spirit, activate Yourself in my life. Give me opportunities to serve and be a blessing to others at my place of work. I am anointed and gifted to do what I do. I make a difference. The anointing upon my life makes a difference.

God, place Your anointing upon me. God, I need You. Enhance my talents, skills, and gifts to accomplish my assignments. Grant me wisdom in all that I do. Help me manage my time, responsibilities, and interactions with others effectively. The workplace is better because God placed me here. I use my influence and power for Jesus. I am mentally and physically sharp. I do more because God is with me. I distinguish myself with an excellent spirit. I am detailed, dependable, and diligent, and I possess a great attitude. I am a valuable asset, bringing excellent and exceptional contributions to the work environment. I shine as a bright light in a dark world. I put my best foot forward and commit to a job well done. I am faithful in small things.

You have knit me and my spouse together in purpose and power. Therefore, my spouse and I commit ourselves and our marriage to be a mighty instrument upon the earth that You designed us to be. My desire is for us to be an example of Your love to our family and friends, associates, and congregants.

Scriptures: Ps. 75:6-7; Mark 9:23; Dan. 5:12; Dan. 1:8-12; Deut. 8:17-18; Dan. 6:3; Col. 3:23-24; Acts 10:34; 1 Cor. 12: 7-11

Receive Jesus As Your Savior

Accepting Jesus as your personal Lord and Savior will be the best decision you can make with your life.

Scripture says, *"If you openly declare that Jesus is Lord and believe in your heart that God raised him from the dead, you will be saved. For it is by believing in your heart that you are made right with God, and it is by openly declaring your faith that you are saved. As the Scriptures tell us, "Anyone who trusts in him will never be disgraced." For "Everyone who calls on the name of the Lord will be saved (Rom. 10:9-13)."*

Pray out loud:

"God, our heavenly Father, you said anyone who confesses You as Lord and Savior and believes in their heart that You raised Him from the dead shall be saved. I confess You as my Lord and Savior. I ask you to forgive me of all my sins and come into my heart. I am saved by faith, cleansed by faith, and made a new creature in Jesus Christ by faith. Thank you, Father, in Jesus' Name. Amen."

Congratulations! I encourage you to find and join a Bible-believing, Bible-teaching church where you can experience exponential growth. I recommend Faith City

Central. You can learn more about them by visiting their website: https://faithcitycentral.org/

Receive the Holy Spirit

After accepting Jesus Christ as your personal Lord and Savior, you need to be equipped and empowered by the Holy Spirit. The following scriptures support receiving the Holy Spirit's indwelling.

Acts 1:8

New King James Version

"But you shall receive power when the Holy Spirit has come upon you, and you shall be witnesses to Me in Jerusalem, and in all Judea and Samaria, and to the end of the earth."

Luke 11:9-13

New King James Version

"So, I say to you, ask, and it will be given to you; seek, and you will find; knock, and it will be opened to you. For everyone who asks receives, and he who seeks finds, and to him who knocks, it will be opened...How much more will *your* heavenly Father give the Holy Spirit to those who ask Him!"

Now, all you have to do is ask, receive, and believe that you receive.

Pray Out Loud:

"Father, I need to be equipped and empowered by Your Holy Spirit. I ask you to fill me with the Holy Spirit with the evidence of speaking in other tongues. According to Luke 11:9-13, you said, "Ask, and it will be given to anyone who asks and who receives." Father, I thank you that I am now filled and baptized with Your Holy Spirit with the evidence of speaking in other tongues. Amen."

After you pray, take a deep breath, make a sound with your voice, move your tongue and lips, and speak your heavenly language. Syllables will rise up from within you. Because you asked in faith, believe that you received regardless of whether you spoke today (Mark 11:24).

Biblical Sources

Unless otherwise noted, all scriptures are taken from https://www.biblegateway.com/ and include scriptures from the following biblical versions:

- Amplified Bible (AMP)
- Amplified Bible, Classic Edition (AMPC)
- Common English Bible (CEB)
- Contemporary English Version (CEV)
- Easy-to-Read Version (ERV)
- EasyEnglish Bible (EASY)
- English Standard Version (ESV)
- Living Bible (TLB)
- The Message (MSG)
- New American Standard Bible (NASB)
- New International Version (NIV)
- New King James Version (NKJV)
- New Living Translation (NLT)
- The Voice (VOICE)

References

https://www.nhsinform.scot/illnesses-and-conditions/a-to-z/
https://www.mayoclinic.org/healthy-lifestyle/fitness/expert-answers/exercise/faq-2005
https://kingjamesbibledictionary.com/Dictionary/walk
https://www.webmd.com/healthy-aging/features/longevity-foods
https://www.nhlbi.nih.gov/news/2023/good-hydration-linked-longevity#:
https://mcpress.mayoclinic.org/healthy-aging/how-quality-sleep-impacts-your-lifespan/#:

Books by Dr. Digna Wheatley Pearson

- Elevation: Empowering and Equipping the Church for Excellence By Creating A Coaching Culture and Using High-Reliability Principles
- Crown of Life Confessions
- Anchored in Hope: Good Grief Devotional Journal

About the Author

Dr. Digna Wheatley Pearson is a licensed minister at Faith City Central, where she has served for over 18 years. A native of the United States Virgin Islands, Digna is a woman after God's heart who chooses to embrace God's plans for her life by devoting her time and energy to serving others.

Digna combines her passion for God with a distinguished healthcare career. She has been a registered nurse in the healthcare industry for over twenty years. Digna brings nearly sixteen years of invaluable experience in Quality, Patient Relations, Risk Management, and Regulatory Affairs at Johns Hopkins Health System. She currently serves as a driving force, making valuable contributions to Service Excellence, specifically in the realm of Patient Experience. She is also a certified professional in healthcare risk management. Digna holds a Doctorate in Strategic Leadership from Regent University with a concentration in Leadership Coaching, a Master's in Biblical and Theological Studies from Dallas Theological Seminary, a Master of Health Administration, a Bachelor of Science in Nursing, and a Bachelor of Arts in Health Administration from the University of Maryland.

In her native hometown, a high school gymnasium proudly bears her name, honoring her leadership in spearheading a march for educational equality. This march resulted in the construction of 12 classrooms, a gymnasium, a bus shed, a track and field, the purchase of textbooks, and the recruitment of teachers.

Dr. Wheatley-Pearson resides in the beautiful state of Maryland. Her daughter, Taylor, a healthcare attorney, is the absolute love of her life.

Contact Information

Website: https://www.dignifiedsolutionz.com/
Email: dignifiedsolutionz@gmail.com

www.ingramcontent.com/pod-product-compliance
Ingram Content Group UK Ltd.
Pitfield, Milton Keynes, MK11 3LW, UK
UKHW020245240426
12048UKWH00026B/1612